★

TEXAS STATE CEMETERY

JASON WALKER & WILL ERWIN

with HELEN THOMPSON

PHOTOGRAPHS BY
LAURENCE PARENT

ADDITIONAL PHOTOGRAPHS BY **WILL ERWIN**   EPILOGUE BY **GOVERNOR RICK PERRY**

UNIVERSITY OF TEXAS PRESS ⚐ AUSTIN

Publication of this work was made
possible in part by support from
Clifton and Shirley Caldwell and a
challenge grant from the National
Endowment for the Humanities.

Requests for permission to reproduce material from
this work should be sent to:
   Permissions
   University of Texas Press
   P.O. Box 7819
   Austin, TX 78713-7819
   www.utexas.edu/utpress/about/bpermission.html

♾ The paper used in this book meets the minimum
requirements of ANSI/NISO Z39.48-1992 (R1997)
(Permanence of Paper).

LIBRARY OF CONGRESS CATALOGING-
IN-PUBLICATION DATA

Walker, Jason, 1975–
   Texas State Cemetery / Jason Walker and Will Erwin
with Helen Thompson ; epilogue by Governor Rick
Perry ; photographs by Laurence Parent ; additional
photographs by Will Erwin. — 1st ed.
      p.   cm. — (Clifton and Shirley Caldwell Texas
heritage series ; no. 16)
   Includes bibliographical references and index.
   ISBN 978-0-292-72672-7 (cloth : alk. paper)
   1. Texas State Cemetery (Austin, Tex.) 2. Texas State
Cemetery (Austin, Tex.)—Pictorial works. 3. Austin
(Tex.)—Genealogy. 4. Austin (Tex.)—Biography.
5. Registers of births, etc.—Texas—Austin. 6. Texas—
Genealogy. 7. Texas—Biography. 8. Registers of births,
etc.—Texas. I. Erwin, Will, 1976– II. Thompson,
Helen A. III. Parent, Laurence. IV. Title.
   F394.A962T489   2011
   929´.3764—dc22

                              2011008979

IN REMEMBRANCE

---

*Kids can come out here and in one day learn more
about Texas history than in a whole semester in class.*

—LIEUTENANT GOVERNOR BOB BULLOCK

CONTENTS

Photograph by Will Erwin

FOREWORD

The Texas State Cemetery in Austin contains the legends, stories, and remains of some of the most famous Texans. You can sense the weight of history and the myriad of stories—told and untold—in the very air above the twenty-one-acre plot located in east Austin.

Unlike many plots of land recognized with a marker or commemorative plaque around Texas, the Cemetery was not the site of a historic event. No battles were fought on its gently sloping hills, no august documents were signed there, no raids were planned, and no political plots were hatched. The Cemetery is a place of rest, which is what makes it interesting.

Those who fought in great battles, settled historic treaties, and wrote the laws that all Texans live by are at rest in the Cemetery. Their stories are what make this place unique. Great soldiers and great politicians lie alongside scoundrels and rogues, all of whom made Texas what it is today. Honored saints and honored sinners find a place within the Cemetery gates. Stephen F. Austin, the "Father of Texas" and a saint by Texas standards, is buried within feet of men known for fighting bloody duels, scalping Comanches, and committing other acts of violence.

It is a great responsibility and honor to serve the State of Texas as members of the Texas State Cemetery Committee. The three of us, plus our superintendent and his staff, consider ourselves guardians of the essential Texas history that permeates this hallowed ground. From the lowest-ranking Confederate veterans to the generals, from the former governors to the athletes, from the statesmen to the educators, they all deserve the respect and honor that we strive daily to give them.

The task of commemorating the Cemetery in a book has been a daunting one for the staff and for us. When the grave of Stephen F. Austin lies within sight of that of Congresswoman Barbara Jordan, which is close to the resting place of Governor John Connally, it's difficult to know where to start and where to stop the story. We have tried to capture the essence of a very special, hallowed place, and the only fault in this effort, we fear, will be the wonderful stories not included. Perhaps that bodes well for another book.

This book is an attempt to make Texans familiar with those heroes and scoundrels at rest in the Cemetery—for their stories are the stories of Texas. Their decisions, good and bad, are what make Texans who they are today. Headstones stand like final testaments, each listing accomplishments and deeds showing the person's worthiness to be buried at the Cemetery. Each is a shrine to public service and devotion to Texas and an invitation to those who visit the grounds to learn about their past.

However, Austin is a long way for many Texans to drive to see the Cemetery. This book is an effort to tell the story of this place to a wider audience than schoolchildren and tour groups. It includes many photographs of the Cemetery, but the book is mainly the story of those buried within its grounds. Some names are instantly recognizable—Stephen F. Austin, Bob Bullock, Barbara Jordan—and others are not so well known, such as Willie Wells, Gideon Lincecum, and May Peterson Thompson. Their stories are told in a broad sense to give readers a taste of their lives. Not much new historical ground is being broken within this book; rather, it is a compendium of notable Texans at the Cemetery. The text is broken down into chapters, some historical in origin and others more of a description or a category. Each chapter is introduced by a modern-day analogue of each category.

We begin at the beginning, a history of the Cemetery itself, the twenty-one-acre plot of land east of the Capitol that was once described by a journalist as a "bleak and rocky hillside."

The next chapter discusses the founding fathers of Texas, the men who served in the Republic of Texas and fought for its independence, as well as the woman considered the "Betsy Ross of Texas." Dr. Gregg Cantrell, historian and author of *Stephen F. Austin, Empresario of Texas*, introduces this chapter, which includes the stories of Austin, Edwin Waller, Thomas William "Peg Leg" Ward, Robert Potter, Josiah Wilbarger, Joel Walter Robison, James Austin Sylvester, and Joanna Troutman.

The following chapter deals with the Civil War and Reconstruction and opens with an introduction by General Hal Hornburg (USAF, ret.), former commander, Air Combat Command. The Cemetery has ten Civil War–era generals buried within the grounds, including nine Confederate and one Union general. Perhaps the most notable is General Albert Sidney Johnston, who was killed at the Battle of Shiloh. Johnston served in the Republic of Texas Army and the US Army before volunteering for the Confederacy. Francis Richard Lubbock, former Texas governor and aide to Confederate President Jefferson Davis, is also included in this chapter, as are Augustus Buchel, soldier of six different armies, and the detested Reconstruction governor, Edmund J. Davis.

Introduced by Don Evans, former US secretary of commerce, the next chapter is dedicated to various public officials, men and women of very different backgrounds and callings who served the public trust. The first man featured in this chapter is Edward Burleson, a vice president of the Republic of Texas and the first man buried at the State Cemetery. Others discussed in this section are Barbara Jordan, Bob Bullock, Ma and Pa Ferguson, James Pinckney Henderson, Allan Shivers, John Connally, and Ann Richards.

In addition to Texans whose burials and applications are automatic—statewide-elected officials for the most part—notable Texans from just about any walk of life can be buried at the State Cemetery. This includes artists, astronauts, sports figures, educators, and law enforcement officers. Notable author Stephen Harrigan opens the chapter dedicated to cultural figures. Harrigan introduces several writers, including J. Frank Dobie, author of *Rattlesnakes* and *The Longhorns*; Fred

Gipson, author of *Old Yeller*; and Thomas Calloway Lea, author and artist. Two other notable cultural figures included in this section are May Peterson Thompson, world-renowned opera soprano and wife of Texas Railroad Commissioner Ernest O. Thompson, and Willie "El Diablo" Wells, Hall of Fame baseball player.

Appropriately, Dr. Steven Weinberg introduces the chapter on Texas educators. Weinberg was awarded the Nobel Prize in Physics in 1979. Originally from New York, he moved to Texas in 1982 to join the University of Texas at Austin as the Jack S. Josey-Welch Foundation Regents Chair in Science, and found the Theory Group of the Physics Department. Weinberg introduces the biographies of Ashbel Smith, the "Father of Texas Medicine"; Gideon Lincecum, naturalist and correspondent with Charles Darwin; Werdner Page Keeton, dean of the University of Texas School of Law; and Walter Prescott Webb, historian and author of *The Texas Rangers*.

No book about Texas would be complete without mentioning the Texas Rangers. The State Cemetery is home to more than forty Texas Rangers, and one of the best-known modern-day Rangers, Captain Jack O'Day Dean, introduces this chapter, which includes William Alexander Anderson "Bigfoot" Wallace, Robert McAlpin Williamson (aka "Three-Legged Willie"), and John Hughes, who signified the end of an era for the Rangers.

This book is by no means a complete register of those who are buried in the Texas State Cemetery. It is not even a list of all the notable Texans here, but it is meant to be an invitation to all Texans to visit and learn about their history, from our founding era during the Republic of Texas, through the wars and tragedies of our past, right through to the most recent folks buried here. We have Civil War soldiers, public officials, cultural leaders, educators, writers, and athletes. They represent a plethora of political beliefs and every economic station.

We have within our grounds the spirit and the range of Texas history, and we honor and respect all those buried there as members of the Texas family that they have shaped, molded, and influenced. Their stories are as broad and diverse as the people of Texas. We hope this book and its pictures capture the soul that lives strongly and loudly in a cemetery in Austin dedicated to the people who made Texas so Texas.

The images by Texas photographer Laurence Parent showcase well the nobility of the grounds and monuments. He is well known for his documentation of famous Texas landscapes. The historical photos, taken by various artists, most unknown, graphically depict our evolution as a cemetery.

The time and effort it has taken our staff has been a labor of love long in the making. They have spent years compiling stories and pictures and checking facts, all the while managing an active, growing cemetery that serves the people of Texas every day. Tours of the Cemetery are available during the week, and it is our hope that this book will inspire you to visit, to enjoy the natural beauty of the site, and to honor the dead who made the Lone Star State what it is. Perhaps it will even give you a glimpse of what we will be.

Maintaining a first-class cemetery is no easy task. With a dedicated staff that makes all of us look good, we are able to meet the demands placed upon the

Cemetery. But without our friends, we would find the job impossible. We owe a great debt of gratitude to Governor Rick Perry, Lieutenant Governor David Dewhurst, and Speaker Joe Straus. Those leaders, along with the members of the Texas House and Senate, provide us with the leadership and funding necessary to preserve history and respect the departed. We also owe a great deal to the Friends of the Texas State Cemetery, a nonprofit organization that enables the Cemetery to function so well, in so many ways. We are thankful to have such friends.

We are privileged to serve our state and its history as members of the Texas State Cemetery Committee and as its superintendent. We hope you will enjoy this book, as we have enjoyed working with the University of Texas Press to bring it to you.

Scott Sayers, CHAIRMAN
Coley Cowden, MEMBER
Borah Van Dormolen, MEMBER
Harry Bradley, SUPERINTENDENT
TEXAS STATE CEMETERY COMMITTEE

ACKNOWLEDGMENTS

Writing a book is a daunting and humbling task. When we took on this project to chronicle the history of the Texas State Cemetery, we didn't quite realize how much time and effort would be necessary to create a manuscript of this kind. We are indeed grateful to the many people who assisted us.

When the idea about a book on the Cemetery was first suggested, we wanted to involve the plot holders, so we came up with the idea of asking some of them to write the introductions to each chapter. We are indebted to Dr. Gregg Cantrell, General Hal Hornburg, Secretary Don Evans, Stephen Harrigan, Dr. Steven Weinberg, Captain Jack O'Day Dean, and Governor Rick Perry for taking time out of their busy schedules to contribute to this book.

Many other plot holders contributed anecdotes, stories, and descriptions of their personal feelings about the Cemetery, and we thank them for their time and effort.

We would like to thank several members of these individuals' staffs: Evan McLaughlin, Kasey Pipes, and Sarah Beaufait from Secretary Don Evans's office, and Deputy Communications Director Ted Royer and Communications Director Andrew Barlow in Governor Rick Perry's office.

Photographs are an important part of this book, and we would like to thank several research institutions for their generosity in supplying historical images for our project: John Anderson, preservation officer, Texas State Library and Archives; Christina Stopka, Deputy Director of Operations, and Judy Shofner, librarian, Texas Ranger Hall of Fame, Waco, Texas; Martha McLain, Daughters of the Republic of Texas; Isaac Lopez, director, Adair Margo Gallery, El Paso, Texas; Michelle Ryden, registrar, El Paso Museum of Art; Lindsey Bloch, photo archivist, Texas State Preservation Board; and Anne Cook, photo librarian, Texas Department of Transportation. We also thank the UT Center for American History, the Austin History Center, and the Tarleton Law Library at the University of Texas School of Law. Stella Wells and Terry Peterson Rodriguez also contributed images. David Morris and Pat Vardell of the Texas Department of Transportation assisted with the map of the Cemetery.

Thanks are also due to Debbie Rothberger, Cemetery Office Manager, for always keeping a positive attitude during the rough patches. And thanks to Mark Swanson for contributing valuable research and thoughts.

We would especially like to thank the University of Texas Press and Bill Bishel, Allison Faust, Lynne Chapman, and Derek George for their interest in publishing the first definitive book on the Texas State Cemetery. We are grateful to them for their patience in answering our many questions about the process.

Our biggest debt of gratitude is owed to the Cemetery Committee, particularly Chairman Scott Sayers, Coley Cowden, Borah Van Dormolen, as well as the Cemetery Superintendent Harry Bradley, who allowed us to devote our attention full-time to this book project.

TEXAS

—★—

STATE

—

CEMETERY

PROLOGUE

This book is a chronicle of the Texas State Cemetery, a museum of history unlike any other in the state. There have been many stories about the Cemetery since it was established in 1851. Many are true, some fabricated, and some hybrid, but all are interesting and entertaining. A burial ground for Texas leaders who helped define our state, the Cemetery has changed over the years, but essentially remains the same as it was in 1851. There are new buildings, tours for visitors, and other additions caused by time. But it is still a cemetery. It is my hope that it will always remain just like it is today—a treasure for Texas.

The best time to visit the Cemetery is early on a spring morning just as the sun is rising. The eastern light illuminates a panoramic view of the history of Texas. You can see and feel some things at that early hour that might be missing later in the day. It is a serene time. The headstones and the inscriptions seem to mean more, and there is a completeness about the Cemetery. Each morning when we open the gates, I usually reflect on the day Lieutenant Governor Bob Bullock sent me to the Cemetery. It was in need of repair and he had a plan to restore it to its original grandeur. The restoration took three years. Most of what was done has proved to be worthy. A small part of the work needed to be corrected, which is normal in restoration projects, but the Cemetery is definitely a better place today than it was in 1994 when the work began.

During those years, I've been privileged to age with the Cemetery. I have a different feeling today than when I started. Maybe it is out of respect, maybe it is just age, or maybe, after all of the funerals and honorary events I've experienced, there is just a greater sense of appreciation for Texas. I've seen many different and interesting people since I began. People who buried their best friend, people who buried a Texas giant, and people who were political enemies all coming here for the final good-bye. There is finality at the Cemetery during a funeral. I once heard it remarked that no matter who is being buried—whether it is a governor, judge, senator, or someone who may not have been as well known—there is one thing certain. On funeral day, the ground is level for all of us. At each funeral you get that feeling: that it is the end of a life and of a contribution of work to Texas. No matter what we've done, we see life complete on that day.

Most of the things I've experienced at the Cemetery are good. Sometimes, though, because of tragedy, there is pain and sadness and, in some cases, suffering. In Viktor Frankl's book *Man's Search for Meaning*, which chronicles his days in a German concentration camp, he writes about experiencing sadness, disappointment, and suffering, all of which are common to a funeral service. Dr. Frankl developed the theory of how, even in our darkest moments, we can gain meaning and encouragement to keep going. He wrote, "There is meaning in suffering." I've seen this happen at a funeral. In some of the saddest moments during a service, I've seen families and friends gain strength from the memories of the deceased and vow to carry on. It is heartwarming and inspirational. It gives definition to the way the Cemetery is special. It's not just a place to hold a funeral.

The Texas State Cemetery is, and always will be, a place of history. But, it is also a place of hope and encouragement. Frankl wrote, "For life to be worth living you must turn outside of yourself and help others." This is what I see at the Cemetery each day. It is a place of memories and sometimes sadness. But, it is also a place where people reach out and help others in their time of need. This shows the true greatness of the Texas State Cemetery.

Harry Bradley
SUPERINTENDENT, TEXAS STATE CEMETERY

I

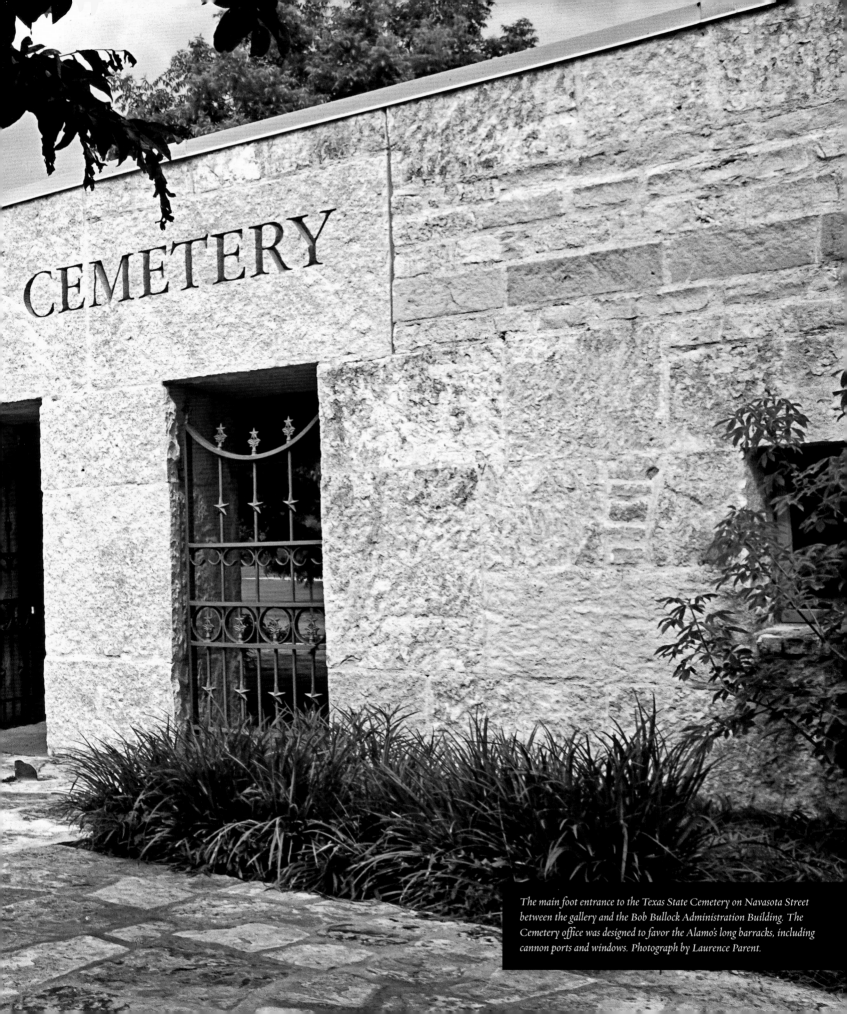

The main foot entrance to the Texas State Cemetery on Navasota Street between the gallery and the Bob Bullock Administration Building. The Cemetery office was designed to favor the Alamo's long barracks, including cannon ports and windows. Photograph by Laurence Parent.

A walkway from a pedestrian gate in the northwest portion of the Cemetery leading to the gallery and the George Christian Reception Room. A room was constructed for grieving family members in 2002 and named for Christian, one of the first Cemetery Committee members, in 2004. Photograph by Laurence Parent.

The Columbarium Wall on the north side of the Cemetery grounds. The ashes of honored Texans can be interred in the Columbarium Wall. The wall was added to the Cemetery grounds during the 1994–1997 renovations. Photograph by Laurence Parent.

A view of State Highway 165, also known as the Louis W. Kemp Highway, toward the Rose Gate entrance to the Texas State Cemetery. SH 165 is a working state highway and accepts vehicle traffic from both the Rose Gate and Comal Street. Photograph by Laurence Parent.

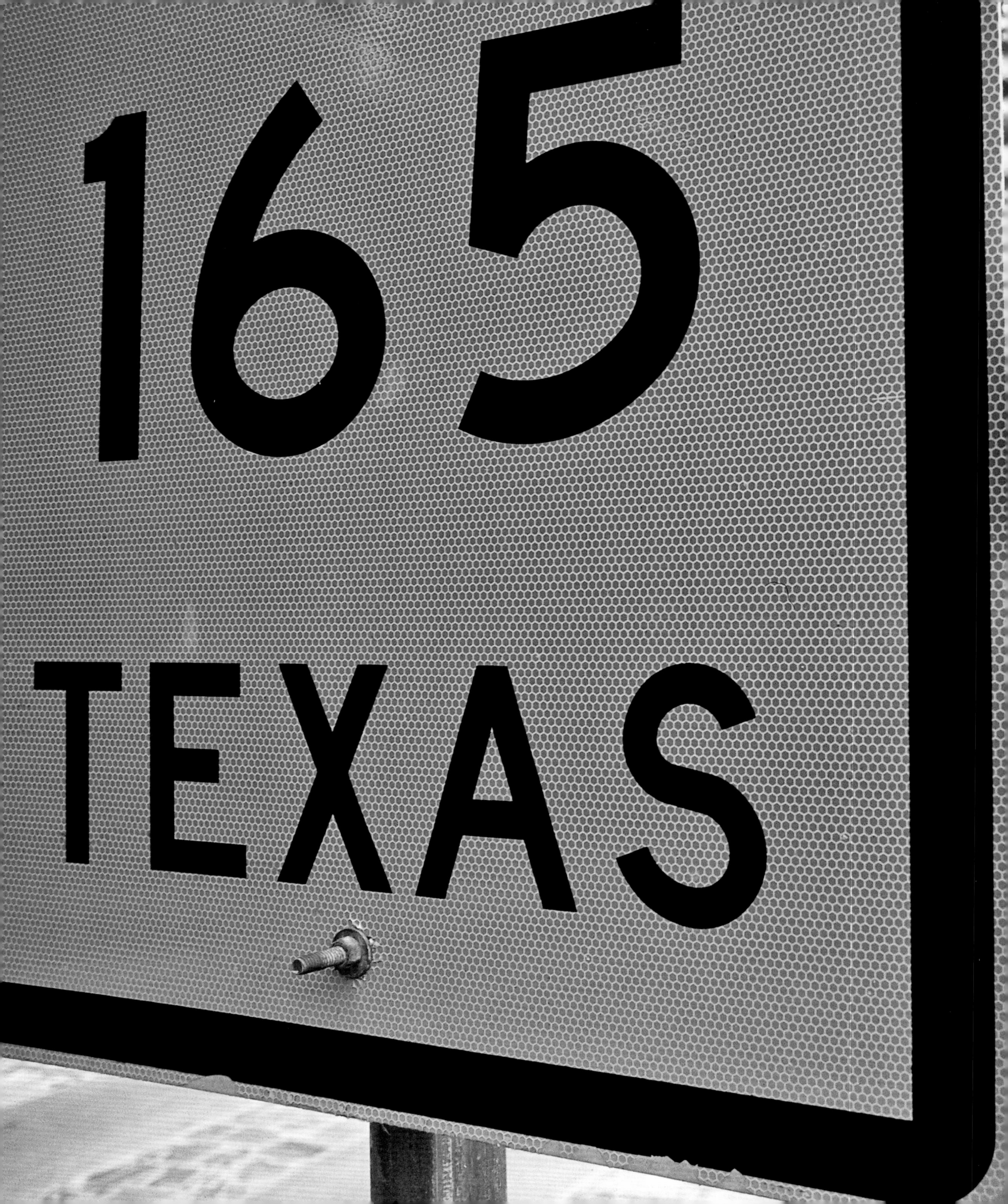
165
TEXAS

State Highway 165 is the main road through the State Cemetery.
Many walking paths branch off of the highway, allowing pedestrians to
stroll through the historic grounds. Photograph by Laurence Parent.

One of the many flower beds at the Texas State Cemetery and Confederate Field beyond. Confederate Field holds the remains of more than 2,000 Confederate veterans and their widows. Most, if not all, of the Confederate veterans buried in Confederate Field did not die during the war but were at some point wards of the State of Texas at the Confederate Men's Home in Austin. Photograph by Laurence Parent.

ARMY
&
ARMY AIR CORPS

NAVY
&
MARINE CORPS

AIR FORCE

THE MEDAL OF HONOR IS THE
HIGHEST AWARD FOR VALOR ABOVE
AND BEYOND THE CALL OF DUTY
THAT THE NATION CAN BESTOW ON
A MEMBER OF THE ARMED FORCES
OF THE UNITED STATES.

THIS MONUMENT INCLUDES THE
NAMES OF RECIPIENTS OF THE
MEDAL OF HONOR WHO WERE
BORN IN TEXAS, ENTERED
MILITARY SERVICE IN TEXAS, OR
ENGAGED IN ACTION IN TEXAS.

MEDAL OF HONOR

The Medal of Honor monument at the Texas State Cemetery commemorates Texans who have been awarded the Congressional Medal of Honor. The monument was dedicated in 1999 by Governor George W. Bush. The monument was the first of many to be dedicated on the Cemetery grounds to Texans who served their country. Photograph by Laurence Parent.

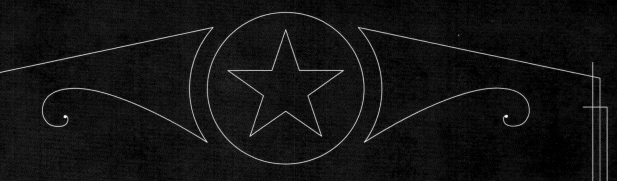

Photograph by Will Erwin

CHAPTER ONE

———

HISTORY

★

OF THE

★

CEMETERY

———

T he Texas State Cemetery is a microcosm of the state. Its existence was originally based on a good idea, even if the well-intentioned donor was overly optimistic about his title to the land. Since its inception, the Cemetery has had its ups and downs, has slid into disrepair, and has been repaired and renovated. The course of its history has reflected the state's own path to an identity.

In the Cemetery are buried heroes, soldiers, artists, politicians, and others of Texas's best and brightest. Now renovated and proudly maintained, the State Cemetery is a showplace of the course of Texas history—a place where anyone can walk through and see the character of the state unfold before his or her eyes.

The Texas State Cemetery was established by an act of the Texas Legislature in the winter of 1851, following the death of one of the state's founding fathers. Edward Burleson was a soldier and commander of troops at the Battle of San Jacinto, vice president of the Republic of Texas, a founder of the city of San Marcos, and an early settler of Waterloo. He died of pneumonia on December 26, 1851, while still serving as president pro tem of the Texas Senate.

As a sign of respect for Burleson, the Texas Senate and Texas House of Representatives devoted their proceedings to eulogizing him. Representative Jason Wilson of Lamar County was one of several lawmakers to comment on Burleson's role in the history of Texas:

From the date of his arrival in Texas to this the hour of his death, the history of Edward Burleson is the history of Texas. There is no page in her annals which does not register his name. There is no event in her progress, in which he is not either a leader or active participant. Intimately connected with the darkest and brightest hours of her destiny, he has emerged from the darkness with no cloud upon his fame; he has basked in the full noontide of her prosperity—a prosperity which he, as much as any man, contributed to bring about—with no feeling of triumph or elevation except for his country.[1]

Arrangements for Burleson's funeral were entrusted to ten Texas senators and representatives. Originally, the committee intended to hold Burleson's funeral at Oakwood Cemetery, the city's most prominent burial ground. Oakwood is the final resting place of such Texas heroes as Alamo survivor Susanna Dickinson; numerous Texas governors, including O. B. Colquitt, James Stephen Hogg, and Oran Roberts; and other notable Texans and Austinites.

The concept that Texas's founders and luminaries deserved their own cemetery was introduced at the meeting attended by the ten committee members. Senator T. H. Duggan made a motion to locate and establish a new "state burying ground." The motion passed, with Representative Andrew Jackson Hamilton (a future Texas governor) offering to donate a tract of land east of the Capitol for Burleson's grave and a future cemetery.

Two days after Burleson's death, a procession left the Capitol bearing the soldier's body to the new state burying ground. The momentous occasion was attended by Texas's most important leaders—members and officers of the Senate; the speaker of the House of Representatives; members of the House; members of the local

One of the oldest known photographs of the Texas State Cemetery, probably taken before 1920. The lack of other monuments denotes the photograph's age. PICA 03151, Austin History Center, Austin Public Library.

Masonic fraternity; and federal, state, and county judges, as well as Governor Peter Bell and other dignitaries.

A few loose ends remained after the funeral, including placing a marker over Burleson's grave. It may not have been until 1854 that the legislature allocated a thousand dollars for a "tomb over the grave of General Edward Burleson." A further allocation of three thousand dollars in 1856 may have accounted for the gray and white marble headstone that now stands over the grave.

Also left to be resolved was the actual title to the land donated by Hamilton. Deed records in Travis County and in the General Land Office suggested that Hamilton might not have owned the land he so generously offered. Despite the controversy, the state acquired the property in 1854 by an act of the legislature, but it wasn't until 1897 that the deed was finally filed with the General Land Office.

The state quickly moved on plans to relocate the remains of other Texas heroes to the burying ground. A few weeks following the Burleson funeral in 1852, the legislature passed a joint resolution to move the remains of Stephen F. Austin to the "Texas State Cemetery," which was the first time the title was used.

However, Austin's remains weren't moved until 1910, and Burleson remained the lone occupant of the Cemetery for four years. In 1856, Abner Smith Lipscomb—a lawyer, War of 1812 veteran, secretary of state during the Mirabeau B. Lamar administration, and Texas Supreme Court justice—died and was buried near Burleson's grave, on a hill at the south end of the property.

After another five years, Burleson and Lipscomb were joined by Forbes Britton and John Caffery Walker. Britton, a West Point graduate and veteran of the Indian Wars and the Mexican War, was senator from the Nueces district in the Seventh (1857–1858) and Eighth (1859–1860) Texas Legislatures, where as a moderate and a Union sympathizer he supported Governor Sam Houston. Britton also was the father-in-law of Edmund J. Davis, the controversial governor of Texas. Walker, a state representative from Harris County, died in 1861, the same year as Britton, and was interred at the Cemetery close to Burleson's and Lipscomb's graves.

Burleson, Lipscomb, Walker, and Britton were to be the last of the Texas forefathers without a military connection to the Civil War to be buried in the Cemetery. They also share the distinction of having the Cemetery be the location of their original burial. Many of the other early inhabitants of the Cemetery were moved from other gravesites.

One of the first to be reinterred was John Hemphill, who died in Richmond, Virginia. He was the first of many Confederate veterans and lawmakers to find a final resting place at the Texas State Cemetery. Hemphill was the first sitting chief justice of the Supreme Court of Texas and a representative to the Congress of the Confederate States of America.

Another early Texas leader to be buried at the Cemetery was Augustus Buchel. Buchel was a veteran of several foreign armies, having fought for the Ottoman Empire and in the Mexican-American War and the Civil War. He died in 1864 at Pleasant Hill, Louisiana, where he was serving as an acting brigadier general in the Confederate Army during the Red River Campaign. The graves of two other Confederate generals, William Read Scurry and Benjamin J. McCulloch, are also at the Cemetery.

Perhaps the most famous of all Confederate generals to be buried at the Cemetery is Albert Sidney Johnston. Johnston was born in Kentucky but was incontrovertibly connected to Texas through his service with the Republic of Texas Army, where he served as first adjutant general and as secretary of war under President Lamar. After his death at the Battle of Shiloh, Johnston was buried in New Orleans. But in January 1867, the Texas Legislature voted to have Johnston's remains transferred to Austin for burial in the State Cemetery.

The episode became a lightning rod in post–Civil War Texas. Celebrations were planned by civic leaders in Galveston, Houston, and other small towns around the state but were canceled by General Philip Sheridan, who was in charge of Texas during the initial period of Reconstruction. Sheridan announced that there was to be no fanfare for Johnston as his body was transferred to Austin. Texans defied Sheridan's prohibition and lined the streets and the railroad tracks between Houston and Austin.

Johnston's casket arrived in Austin without incident, and the Civil War hero was laid to rest at the foot of the hill where Burleson and other early Texas leaders were buried. Johnston would again become the focus of attention at the turn of the twentieth century when the United Daughters of the Confederacy gave the leader a grander monument.

As the years passed, it became obvious that more than just land was required to make the Cemetery a place of honor. No arrangements had been made by the legislature to deal with the Cemetery's maintenance, and no rules defined who could be buried there. In 1866, some of the problems were addressed by the legislature, which voted to authorize the governor to appoint a sexton to oversee the grounds and fifteen hundred dollars to enclose the southern section. It also became apparent—as more people were buried on the grounds—that measures were needed to identify graves. In 1871, the legislature authorized the sexton to place a permanent marker at the head of each grave not already marked.

But the Cemetery's physical appearance began to receive negative press in the mid-1870s. The March 31, 1874, edition of the *Daily Democratic Statesman* described the grounds unflatteringly, as a "bleak and rocky hillside in Austin," protected only by "a rough and dilapidated picket fence without a solitary tree or bush to break the sod and dreary prospect." Conditions languished for a few more years until finally the sexton of the grounds reported the Cemetery's shortcomings to the legislature in 1879. The next decade saw a few improvements—a new fence and a gate were erected.

Although guidelines establishing eligibility for burial had never been set forth, Confederate veterans seemed to have an early claim on plots at the Cemetery. The first Confederate enlisted man to be buried was Sam Everett. Everett, whose name is spelled "Everet" on his headstone, served in the cavalry regiment Terry's Texas Rangers and was buried at the State Cemetery in 1886.

A period photograph of the monument to Edmund J. Davis that was erected by his brother. C00413, Austin History Center, Austin Public Library.

N-28

Period photo of Republic Hill at the Texas State Cemetery taken between 1930 and 1943 and showing the Stephen F. Austin monument. C03862, Austin History Center, Austin Public Library.

He was one of more than a hundred Confederate veterans to be admitted to the Confederate Home between 1886 and 1888. The State of Texas bought the Confederate Home in 1891, and membership reached more than two thousand Confederate veterans between then and 1953. Of those veterans, more than eighteen hundred were interred at the Cemetery between Everett's death and the mid-twentieth century.

In 1908, the United Daughters of the Confederacy founded the Confederate Woman's Home in Austin for the widows or spouses of Confederate veterans. It is unclear when widows and spouses became eligible for burial at the Cemetery, but more than 350 are buried on the grounds. The last Confederate widow to be laid to rest at the Cemetery was Elizabeth Lusby Kyle. Kyle was born several years after the close of the Civil War, in 1872, and died in 1965.

At almost the same time the first enlisted Confederate soldiers were being buried at the State Cemetery, Federal soldiers were being disinterred from the grounds. It is unclear when US Army soldiers were first buried at the Cemetery; however, starting in the early 1880s, the Quartermaster Corps began closing military bases in the western United States. As these installations closed, soldiers buried at the bases were disinterred and taken to national burial grounds. Confederate soldiers, of course, did not qualify for burial in these cemeteries. Forty-six US Army soldiers were disinterred from the State Cemetery grounds and transported to the US National Cemetery in San Antonio, as were US Army soldiers from around the state.

The Federal graves had always been separate from the rest of the graves on the grounds. While Johnston, McCulloch, Buchel, and the other Confederate generals were buried in the southwest area of the Cemetery, Civil War and Reconstruction-era US Army soldiers were seemingly buried as far away from them as possible, in the northeast corner of the grounds. Today, that corner remains unoccupied except for a single Union soldier: Antonio

A period photograph of the northeast portion of the Texas State Cemetery in the 1930s. The drainage ditch seen running through the central portion of the picture is now a flowing pond that was constructed during the 1994–1997 renovations. This photo was in the possession of Viola Gay Barnes, daughter of a former caretaker at the Cemetery, when it was donated to the Cemetery research staff during the renovations.

Briones, a private in the First Texas Cavalry. Briones, who served in a Union Army unit organized by Edmund J. Davis, was not originally buried at the Cemetery, but was interred in 1998 by his descendents. His remains were disinterred from Austin's Oakwood Cemetery.

Confederate veterans and widows continued to be buried at the Cemetery until the 1960s. The last Confederate veteran interred at the Cemetery was Robert Barnes. Barnes, originally thought to be from Alabama, moved to Texas in 1878, well after the Civil War, to live in the Confederate Home. Like many other residents of the Home, he had moved to Texas after serving in the Confederacy. He died in 1943.

Interest in Albert Sidney Johnston's resting place was rekindled in the state legislature in 1901 when the United Daughters of the Confederacy requested a bigger and more elaborate monument to the general. The legislature appropriated ten thousand dollars for the project, and a committee consisting of Governor Joseph D. Sayers, the superintendent of public buildings and grounds, and the president of the United Daughters of the Confederacy was formed to supervise the details.

Sayers contacted well-known Austin sculptor Elisabet Ney, who was asked to submit a design for the statue. Ney created a memorial featuring the recumbent figure of Johnston. She won the commission and set to work on a plaster mold, which was completed in 1903. It was shipped to Italy to be sculpted in Italian marble. Molds of Ney's sculptures of Sam Houston and Stephen F. Austin were sent at the same time. The completed Johnston, Houston, and Austin sculptures were shipped back to the United States for exhibition at the 1904 St. Louis World's Fair, where the Johnston sculpture captured a bronze medal. Copies of the Austin and Houston sculptures reside in the Texas Capitol with the originals in the US Capitol's National Statuary Hall.

Photograph of the sculpture of Albert Sidney Johnston that covers his grave. The photo was taken in 1970 by a Texas Department of Transportation photographer.

A period shot of Albert Sidney Johnston's grave. PICA 13053, Austin History Center, Austin Public Library.

The sculpture of Johnston arrived in Austin in 1905 and was placed on top of his grave. A Gothic-style chapel was erected around the statue and dedicated on September 27, 1906, at a ceremony attended by former Governor Sayers, Governor Samuel Lanham, and members of the United Daughters of the Confederacy and the Daughters of the Republic of Texas.

Johnston's sculpture has become a centerpiece of the Cemetery, remaining to this day one of its most visited and photographed monuments, alongside those of Stephen F. Austin and Joanna Troutman. The Austin and Troutman statues were cast in bronze by Pompeo L. Coppini, an Italian sculptor who immigrated to Texas in 1901. Statues designed by Coppini are still on prominent display at the University of Texas at Austin, the Capitol grounds, and the Cemetery.

Perhaps spurred by the success of the Johnston memorial and keen to recapture public interest in the state's history, Governor O. B. Colquitt dusted off an idea that had lain dormant since Burleson's death. Colquitt, who had also shown interest in monuments for the Alamo and the San Jacinto battlefields, brought the full weight of his office to bear on restoring Stephen F. Austin's remains to the city named in his honor.

Austin's reinterment was to be the main objective of Colquitt's efforts, but the governor also focused on obtaining the remains of two other early Texas leaders. Since the end of the Civil War, the Cemetery had been a burying ground for Confederate officers and soldiers, but Colquitt wanted the Cemetery to reflect the earlier chapters in Texas history as well. In addition to Stephen F. Austin, Colquitt sought to have Joanna Troutman moved from her place of burial in her native Georgia. Civil War General John Wharton's remains were also to be disinterred from his resting place in Hempstead, Texas.

Austin had been buried on his sister's land at Peach Point in Brazoria County. After arrangements for the reinterment were completed in 1910, Colquitt made a state occasion of Austin's return to the capital. His remains lay in state at the Capitol before being removed to the Cemetery, where Austin was laid to rest at the top of the highest hill near Edward Burleson. Rather than obsessing on just the Civil War, as many Southern states did at the time, Texas officials shifted the focus to another era in the state's history, when it was an independent republic. Thus, the state was able to turn its attentions away from the Civil War—a healing option other former Confederate states did not have.

Joanna Troutman, inspired by the Texas battle for independence, in turn inspired others. She sewed the first Texas flag—and it was also the first to depict the "Lone Star," now so integral to our state's identity. Troutman was reinterred at the State Cemetery in 1913. The text on her monument reads:

> Miss Joanna Troutman then 18 years of age, fired with her love of liberty and the zeal of the volunteer, with her own hands made a beautiful lone star flag and presented it to the Georgia Battalion and they landed in Texas with it in December 1835. The flag was symbolic of the lone struggle Texas was making. The flag was unfurled at Velasco and later carried to Goliad where it proudly waved over the walls of that fortress. This flag was raised as national flag on the walls of Goliad by Fannin when he heard of the Declaration of Texas Independence on March 8, 1836. It was constructed of white silk with an azure star of five points. On one side was the motto "Liberty or Death," and on the reverse side in Latin, "Where Liberty Dwells There Is My Country."

Renewed interest in the Cemetery was a catalyst for improvements to the grounds. No longer a "bleak and rocky hillside in Austin," the Cemetery received a glowing report in 1914 from Ernest R. Barnes, Cemetery sexton from 1912 to 1950. "The present condition of the State Cemetery is better than it had even been before," he wrote. "It is well kept, and due regard has been paid to the sacredness of the ground."[2]

In the 1920s public interest in Texas's Republic past continued to grow. With the 1936 centennial of Texas Independence Day just a few years ahead, the celebration of the event became the pet project of businessman and historian Louis W. Kemp. Kemp discovered that many of the signers of the Texas Declaration of

Independence, as well as former governors and other luminaries, were buried in abandoned graves around Texas. He was horrified at the neglect and took it upon himself to champion the cause of dead and almost-forgotten Texas icons.

Kemp appeared before the Senate to request help. In 1929, Senate Bill 181 was passed calling for "the removal of the remains of prominent Texans from present burial grounds to the State Cemetery in Austin, Texas, for erection of monuments in the State Cemetery, and, in a few instances, erection of monuments at cemeteries where said bodies are now buried."

Between the years of 1929 and 1931, the remains of James Pinckney Henderson, the first governor of Texas; Peter Hansborough Bell, governor and Texas Ranger; David Spangler Kaufman, United States congressman; Robert Potter, signer of the Texas Declaration of Independence; and others were removed from cemeteries around the state and brought to Austin. In all, Kemp would be responsible for more than one hundred reinterments at the State Cemetery by 1935.

But Kemp did not limit his efforts to the reburial of the celebrated dead. He worked tirelessly to see that procedures were put in place that would ensure the physical well-being of the Cemetery. By the 1920s, the Texas Board of Control assumed responsibility for the Cemetery and, with Kemp's encouragement, worked with the State Highway Department to build a road system within the site. This road would prove to be a crucial component to the future welfare of the grounds. The road, which winds through the hills and dales of the Cemetery, was christened the Lou Kemp Highway by the State Highway Department in tribute to Kemp's hard work. The Highway Department designated the road a state highway through various means by 1939. The designation assured that the road—and the Cemetery—would be eligible for federal funds some sixty years later.

Kemp was effective, but not all of his attempts met with success. In April 1938, believing that all of the necessary arrangements had been made with the city of Potosi, a community that Moses Austin founded in Missouri, Kemp dispatched Austin undertaker Thurlow B.

Weed to bring the senior Austin's remains to the State Cemetery. It was a trip mired in misunderstanding. Weed returned to Austin empty-handed, and the remains of Stephen F. Austin's father have stayed to this day in Potosi.

Louis Kemp died November 15, 1956, in Houston, where he was buried. The next spring, however, Kemp was himself reburied in the State Cemetery on May 5, 1957, beside a granite marker placed there in his honor.

For the Cemetery's first one hundred years, eligibility for burial was informally and somewhat erratically determined. But in 1953, the legislature formalized guidelines for qualifications for burial—eligibility was spelled out, but the superintendent of the Cemetery had the final say.

Today, those eligible for burial are:

1. a former member of the legislature or a member who dies in office;
2. a former elected state official or an elected state official who dies in office;
3. a former state official or a state official who dies in office who has been appointed by the governor and confirmed by the senate and who served at least twelve years in the office to which appointed;
4. a person specified by a governor's proclamation, subject to review and approval by the State Cemetery Committee;
5. a person specified by a concurrent resolution adopted by the legislature, subject to review and approval by the Committee; and
6. a person specified by order of the Committee, only if the Committee finds that the person made a significant contribution to Texas history and culture in the following fields: air and space, agriculture, art and design, business and labor, city building, education, industry, justice, military affairs, law enforcement, oil and gas, performing arts, philanthropy, ranching, religion, science and medicine, sports, and writing.

After Kemp's death, little changed at the Cemetery beyond the continued burials of noteworthy Texans such as Miriam Amanda Wallace "Ma" Ferguson, who

A period photograph of the caretaker's cottage on the grounds of the Texas State Cemetery taken in the 1930s with a cat in the foreground. The picture was likely taken by Viola Gay Barnes, daughter of the Cemetery caretaker at the time.

died in 1961 and was buried next to her husband and fellow governor James Edward "Pa" Ferguson, who died in 1944.

Others buried at the Cemetery during that period were Governor Dan Moody (1966), Texas Ranger Charles Miller (1971), Attorney General Crawford Martin (1972), State Treasurer Jesse James (1977), Speaker of the House Homer Leonard (1979), Texas Ranger George Christopher Brakefield (1982), Governor Allan Shivers (1985), Speaker of the House Thomas Durwood Manford Jr. (1988), Texas Ranger William Wilson (1990), and Speaker of the House and Chief Justice of the Supreme Court of Texas Robert Wilburn Calvert (1994).

It was at the funeral of former Texas House member Harry Whitworth in 1994 that the grounds of the Cemetery came under scrutiny again. Only this time it wasn't a private businessman like Louis Kemp noticing the dilapidated state of the Cemetery, but a powerful elected official. Lieutenant Governor Bob Bullock, attending the Whitworth funeral, was "appalled" at the state of the grounds. Although the Cemetery had a grounds crew that performed regular maintenance, it was, in Bullock's opinion, not nearly enough. The Cemetery was not the place he envisioned it to be. Bullock was inspired by the idea of a complete restoration and beautification of the Cemetery grounds, and it was his goal to make the Cemetery a destination for schoolchildren, a must-visit landmark just as important as the Capitol, the Governor's Mansion, and the Alamo.

At Bullock's instigation, the legislature approved an appropriation for the benefit of the Cemetery, but it was obvious that more creative funding measures would be necessary. The road through the Cemetery had already been designated a state highway in 1939, but it was possible to receive federal grants set aside for the restoration

A 1997 photograph of Governor George W. Bush at the Texas State Cemetery rededication. Bush was governor during the 1994–1997 renovations. Texas State Cemetery Photo Archives.

of historic landmarks. About 80 percent of the renovation project was funded by the federal government.

Bullock installed longtime colleague Harry Bradley as superintendent to oversee the project. The $4.7-million restoration and enhancement project was initiated in 1994 and completed in March 1997. The project was a joint undertaking by the General Services Commission, Texas Parks and Wildlife Department, Texas Department of Transportation, Texas Historical Commission, Lower Colorado River Authority, State Preservation Board, and Texas Department of Criminal Justice. The restoration project, which was developed and generally credited to Bullock, involved the construction of the Visitor Center, the Columbarium Wall, a pond, and the renovation and restoration of the monuments and grounds.

The project involved several new components to enhance public understanding of the state's history.

Inspired by the long barracks of the Alamo, the Visitors Center stands at the main public entrance to the State Cemetery. Exhibitions in the gallery of this building highlight the history of the Cemetery. The Visitors Center also houses administration offices and a maintenance facility for the Cemetery grounds. The Columbarium Wall to the north provides both a ceremonial entrance for state funerals and niches for burial urns in the 150-foot walls that flank either side of the historic central gates.

In addition to these new constructions, each headstone in the Confederate soldiers' sections and Republic Hill was cleaned and repaired. The project was funded by a grant from ISTEA (Intermodal Surface Transportation Efficiency Act of 1991) and the General Services Commission.

In March 1997, a rededication ceremony was held with Governor George W. Bush, Lieutenant Governor

Bob Bullock, Speaker of the House Pete Laney, and other distinguished guests attending.

In the same year, the Texas Legislature established the Texas State Cemetery Committee to oversee operations at the Cemetery. The Committee consists of three members, one chosen by the governor, one by the lieutenant governor, and one by the speaker of the House of Representatives. The first three members were George Christian, Martin Allday, and Ralph Wayne.

Bob Bullock died in 1999. He was buried in one of the most prominent plots on the Cemetery grounds next to the Cemetery's first occupant, Edward Burleson, and in the shadow of Stephen F. Austin's monument.

Since the restoration, Superintendent Harry Bradley has been leading an expanded grounds crew that oversees the regular maintenance of the Cemetery. A research staff includes historians who help maintain exhibits, correspond with plot holders, and conduct tours for schoolchildren.

The Cemetery has become one of the state's premier locations for monuments remembering the vast history of Texas. A monument to the Texans who died in the September 11, 2001, terrorist attacks and in Operation Enduring Freedom in Afghanistan was unveiled in 2003 on the Cemetery grounds. It contains two beams from the wreckage of the World Trade Center. Several monuments have been erected since then, such as the African-American Texas Legislators monument, and a monument dedicated to the American Revolutionary War veterans who later colonized Texas.

The state monument to Texans who died during the September 11, 2001, terrorist attacks in Washington, DC, New York, and Pennsylvania, as well as those Texas soldiers who died during Operation Enduring Freedom in Afghanistan. The monument was picked from many designs and was dedicated by Governor Rick Perry in 2003. O'Connell Robertson and Associates of Austin submitted the design. Photograph by Laurence Parent.

CHAPTER TWO

REPUBLIC

*

OF

*

TEXAS

INTRODUCTION BY DR. GREGG CANTRELL

A view of Section C, or Republic Hill, at the Texas State Cemetery.
Photograph by Laurence Parent.

INTRODUCTION

BY DR. GREGG CANTRELL

Dr. Gregg Cantrell is a professor of history and the Erma and Ralph Lowe Chair in Texas History at Texas Christian University. His second book, Stephen F. Austin, Empresario of Texas, *was published in 1999. It received several awards, including the T. R. Fehrenbach Book Award and the Summerfield G. Roberts Award.*

On March 2, 1836, fifty-nine men assembled in a drafty, unfinished building in the raw frontier village of Washington-on-the-Brazos. All but ten of them had been in Texas for fewer than three months; only two—José Antonio Navarro and José Francisco Ruiz—were native Texans. One by one, they stepped up to a table and signed the Texas Declaration of Independence, giving birth to the Republic of Texas.

Over the next two weeks, the delegates wrote a constitution for the new republic and created an interim government, but independence would still have to be won on the battlefield. Revolution had erupted the previous fall, following the abolition of the Mexican Constitution of 1824 and the centralization of power in the hands of Mexican president Antonio López de Santa Anna. During the six weeks following the Declaration of Independence, the Alamo fell, the garrison at Goliad surrendered and was massacred, and Sam Houston struggled to forge a ragtag army while retreating eastward. The Texas Revolution came to a climax on the afternoon of April 21 when Houston's troops overwhelmed Santa Anna's army at San Jacinto. Santa Anna was captured the next day and he ordered his remaining troops from Texas. Independence was won.

In September 1836, Sam Houston was elected president of the Republic of Texas. The new government faced a daunting task in rebuilding the war-torn country, securing it against Mexican re-invasion and hostile Indians, achieving diplomatic recognition from the world community, and developing the economy. Over the coming decade, the Republic would struggle with all these challenges, achieving them with varying degrees of success.

Mexico refused to acknowledge Texas's independence. Twice in 1842, Mexican armies invaded and briefly occupied San Antonio. In the aftermath of the second of these invasions, Houston dispatched troops to South Texas in pursuit of the Mexicans. Disobeying orders to return home, more than three hundred of the men crossed the Rio Grande and were defeated in battle by a much larger Mexican force. Following their surrender and a subsequent break for freedom, the men were recaptured. On March 25, 1843, seventeen of the prisoners were executed in the infamous "Black Bean Incident," and the survivors were marched to Mexico City and thrown in prison. This incident, and many others, underscored the precarious position of the young republic.

Internal security also posed a serious problem. In East Texas, President Mirabeau B. Lamar, who replaced Houston as president in 1838, waged war on the Cherokees, themselves recent immigrants. Following their defeat at the Battle of the Neches in the summer of 1839, the remaining Cherokees and most of the other East Texas Indians were driven into Oklahoma. On the western frontier, the Comanche Indians (immigrants to Texas in the mid-1700s) terrorized settlers with their brilliant horsemanship and fierce warrior code. In San Antonio in March 1840, thirty-five Comanche and seven Texans were killed when negotiations for the release of captives broke down and a riot ensued. Following this incident (known as the "Council House Fight"), war with the Comanche raged on the frontier until Sam Houston returned to the president's office and brought matters under some semblance of control.

A sculpture of Joanna Troutman, the woman who sewed the first Texas flag to feature the iconic lone star. The sculpture, made by Pompeo Coppini, adorns the top of Troutman's grave. Photograph by Will Erwin.

Grave of the Jack Brothers. William, Spencer, and Patrick all fought for Texas Independence. Buried in Galveston, the state had Louis Kemp move the remains of the Jack Brothers to the Texas State Cemetery in 1942. Photograph by Laurence Parent.

Leaders of the Republic also sought to bring economic stability to the fledgling nation. In 1841, Lamar dispatched the Santa Fe Expedition, which, although intended to open a trade route between Texas and New Mexico, resulted instead in the capture and imprisonment of nearly three hundred Texans by Mexico. The expedition was but one example of Lamar's vision of a Texan version of Manifest Destiny, in which Texas would someday rival the United States as a continental power.

Another example of Lamar's vision was his insistence on locating the Republic's capital at the site of Austin, on the western frontier, far from the centers of Anglo-Texan population. Exposed to Indian and Mexican attacks and difficult to reach, the new capital was a luxury that the republic could scarcely afford, but Lamar envisioned its future as the centrally located seat of a vast Texan empire. The president's grand plans for Texas came at a high cost: under Lamar, the national debt rose from $1 million to $7 million and the currency depreciated drastically.

If the Republic had struggled on the military and economic fronts, it nevertheless became a magnet for immigrants. In a decade the population grew from about forty thousand to nearly one hundred and forty thousand. The Republic made land available practically free to emigrants from the United States, and it also resurrected a version of the Mexican empresario system to attract emigrants from the United States and Europe. In the last years of the Republic, some ten thousand colonists from Kentucky, Indiana, Illinois, and Ohio settled in the E. S. Peters colony in northeast Texas; about seven thousand Germans came to a grant in the hill country; and approximately two thousand French Alsatians settled in Henri Castro's colony southwest of San Antonio. These settlers gave Texas an ethnically diverse population that can still be seen today.

By the time Houston returned to office in 1841, the Republic's financial woes made annexation by the United States more desirable than ever. Texans overwhelmingly desired statehood, but concerns about slavery effectively prevented American action. In 1844, however, James K. Polk won the American presidency on a pro-annexation platform. The outgoing president, John Tyler, viewed it as a mandate for annexation. Having previously failed to gain Senate approval for a treaty of annexation, Tyler proposed annexing Texas by means of a congressional joint resolution requiring only simple majorities in both houses of Congress. It succeeded, and on February 19, 1846, the last president of the Republic of Texas, Anson Jones, lowered the Lone Star flag and raised the Stars and Stripes over the Texas Capitol.

The men and women who created the Republic of Texas saw themselves as the heirs of the American revolutionary heritage. Like their forebears of 1776, they viewed the Texas Revolution as a struggle of liberty against despotism. During Texas's ten years as an independent republic, Texans forged a sense of national identity that set them apart from other Americans while also confirming their beliefs in American values and institutions. This sense of being both Texans and Americans continues to be a source of pride in the twenty-first century.

★

A view of Republic Hill in the snow. Regardless of weather, holidays, or weekends, the State Cemetery's gates are always open between 8 a.m. and 5 p.m. 365 days a year. Photograph by Will Erwin.

No other place in the state represents the Republic of Texas as well as the Texas State Cemetery. Signers of the Texas Declaration of Independence, Goliad survivors, Supreme Court justices, a congressman, and one seamstress all contributed significantly to the founding of the Republic of Texas and are buried at the Cemetery.

STEPHEN FULLER AUSTIN

1793–1836

REPUBLIC HILL, SECTION 1 (C1), ROW L, PLOT 20

Arguably the most famous man to be buried at the Texas State Cemetery was not interred there until many years after his death. Stephen F. Austin was buried in the most prominent location at the Cemetery in 1910 after a state funeral, seventy-four years after his death and fifty-nine years after the Texas Legislature established the Cemetery and expressed their wish to have Austin moved to the city named for him. Austin was a natural fit for the Cemetery, a place of honor for a man who held many titles during his time in Texas and gave so much for its future.

Austin served in many roles in Texas's early history, including "empresario," diplomat to Mexico and the United States, army commander, and finally secretary of state to the Republic of Texas.

Born near lead mining country in southwestern Virginia in 1793 to Moses and Maria Austin, Stephen F. Austin, best known to Texas schoolchildren as the "Father of Texas," fulfilled his father's ambition of bringing Anglo-American settlers to what amounted to the Mexican frontier. In a letter to Major General E. P. Gaines, Austin spoke of his dedication to Texas: "The prosperity of Texas has been the object of my labors, the idol of my existence—it has assumed the character of a religion, for the guidance of my thoughts and actions, for fifteen years."[1]

His father had experience settling frontier areas of the United States. In 1798, the elder Austin moved his family to southeastern Missouri, where he founded the city of Potosi near the lead mines in the area. The younger Austin eventually took over the mining portion of the family business. He served as adjutant of a militia battalion and for several years was a member of the Missouri territorial legislature. Eventually, the Austins' mining interests failed, and he began looking for a new start in Arkansas, where he engaged in land speculation and mercantile activities. Austin did not remain long in Arkansas, but was there long enough to become a district judge.

By 1820 Austin had moved on, this time to Louisiana, where he studied law in New Orleans. At the same time, his father had begun the process of applying to the Mexican government for land grants in the Texas territory. Initially, the younger Austin was skeptical of his father's enterprise, but eventually he helped secure funding for the exploratory trip to San Antonio.

Stephen Fuller Austin, known popularly as the "Father of Texas" to many schoolchildren. His monument is the centerpiece of Republic Hill at the State Cemetery, where many prominent Texas historical figures lie at rest. Prints and Photographs Collection, Austin, Stephen F., file CN 02318, Center for American History, University of Texas at Austin.

STEPHEN.F.
AUSTIN

The grave of Stephen F. Austin is a massive pink granite marker topped by Pompeo Coppini's statue. Austin died in 1836 and was buried on his sister's land at Peach Point before being interred at the State Cemetery in 1910. Photograph by Laurence Parent.

The project soon became solely his venture. After a four-week bout with pneumonia, Moses Austin died June 10, 1821. In his final letter to his son, Moses entreated him to continue efforts to bring colonists to Mexico's northernmost and sparsely inhabited state, Coahuila y Tejas. In pursuit of this goal, Stephen traveled to San Antonio in August 1821 and was allowed by Governor Antonio María Martínez to explore the region between the Brazos and San Antonio Rivers as a possible site for his settlers. Terms were agreed upon, and he returned to New Orleans to make arrangements. The first settlers from the United States arrived in December.

Austin had selected a site on the lower Colorado and Brazos Rivers—an area with rich land and prime for farming. Colonists began building households in the area in early 1822. At the same time, though, Mexico was experiencing political upheaval. It had been in the throes of revolution since 1810 and finally gained independence from Spain in 1822.

The timing spelled trouble for Austin and his settlers. The newly appointed, post-Revolutionary Mexican officials no longer honored the terms he had carefully negotiated for settlement. They refused to acknowledge Moses Austin's grant almost immediately after Anglo-American colonists began to arrive in Texas. To make matters worse, officials in independent Mexico also refused to acknowledge the arrangement because it had been made with officials in the old regime.

Austin traveled to Mexico City to meet with the new Mexican authorities and was successful in his negotiations. The Mexican government soon passed a law that confirmed Austin's right to colonize the land. Austin was designated the new colony's "empresario," or administrative authority.

As empresario, Austin was responsible for a wide range of tasks, including controlling immigration into the region, establishing a judicial and law enforcement system, surveying and allocating land to colonists, and supervising the creation of a basic social infrastructure. Austin also oversaw the building of roads, granaries, and other infrastructure essential to a growing colony, and he acted as a spokesman to the Mexican government for the colonists' interests, which sometimes were not compatible with Mexican law. In 1827, he lobbied successfully against banning slavery in Texas even though it had been illegal in Mexico since 1824.

At the same time, the movement for Texas independence was gaining momentum. Austin, however, was a somewhat reluctant participant in the independence movement; he had always worked through diplomatic channels to resolve issues between colonists and the government. For his stance, Austin was accused of being an "appeaser" and was criticized by fellow Texans eager to establish their own republic. Austin believed in nonviolence, and his compatriots' rush to independence caused him sorrow: "Some men in the world hold the doctrine that it is degrading and corrupt to use policy in anything. . . . There is no degradation in prudence and a well tempered and well timed moderation," Austin wrote shortly before his death.[2]

Austin based his philosophy on previous experience. In 1827, Austin led troops against rebels during the Fredonia Rebellion, assisting Mexican forces to quell the uprising. However, in 1834, he was imprisoned in Mexico City under suspicion of treason, and he remained

A view of Pompeo Coppini's bronze likeness of Stephen F. Austin. Photograph by Laurence Parent.

there until 1835. Austin had participated in the Convention of 1833, in which the settlers drafted a series of petitions to the Mexican government, and this possibly led to suspicions of his loyalty. In 1835, Austin urged Texans to join a Federalist rebellion brewing in Yucatán against President Antonio López de Santa Anna. When the armed Texas Revolution began in earnest in 1835, Austin commanded Texas volunteers for a brief time and then, ever the diplomat, went to the United States to gain support for the Texan cause.

After the 1836 victory of Texan forces over Mexican troops at San Jacinto, General Santa Anna signed the Treaty of Velasco that recognized Texas independence. Austin campaigned for president, but was defeated by war hero Sam Houston. The newly elected president offered Austin the post of secretary of state, which he accepted.

Austin died December 27, 1836, at the age of forty-three. He was buried on his sister's land at Peach Point

in Brazoria County. His remains lay in a family cemetery for decades before being brought to the Texas State Cemetery in 1910 at the behest of Governor O. B. Colquitt. Since the founding of the Cemetery, lawmakers had wanted Austin's remains to be interred in the capital city. On the same day as Edward Burleson's death in 1851, lawmakers passed a resolution providing for the interment of Austin's remains at the State Cemetery. It was not until 1910, however, that their wishes came to fruition. The remains of the Father of Texas were transported from Peach Point to Austin by railroad. A state funeral was held on the Cemetery grounds on October 10, 1910.

Austin's marker is made of unpolished pink granite with bronze lettering, and a bronze statue by Pompeo L. Coppini stands atop the monument. The text on his headstone bears the inscription, "Wise, Gentle, Courageous, and Patient, He was the founder of a mighty commonwealth."

EDWIN WALLER

1800–1881

REPUBLIC HILL, SECTION 1 (C1), ROW T, PLOT 11

The city of Austin owes its place on the map—and most certainly its character—to Edwin Waller. Before 1839, the Republic of Texas was trying to establish itself as a sovereign nation, and Austin was just a small settlement on the Colorado River known as Waterloo. But Texas needed a capital, and, after moving the seat of government several times, the Republic set up a commission to select a permanent location. Despite heavy resistance from Sam Houston, the commission chose Waterloo, and Edwin Waller was put in charge of the planning and construction of the new city. In 1839, Waterloo officially became known as Austin, named in honor of Stephen F. Austin.

Considering that Waterloo had few citizens and even fewer buildings or roads, Waller's task was immense, even putting aside the fact that the town was at the far western frontier of Texas and always under threat of Indian attacks. To make matters worse, Sam Houston vehemently opposed the new location of the capital, preferring instead his namesake city of Houston. In addition to his other duties, Waller had to outmaneuver Houston's frequent attempts to relocate the capital.

But Waller was accustomed to battles of all kinds. Born November 4, 1800, in Spotsylvania County, Virginia, he moved to Texas in 1831. Soon after, he became a hero to Texans as the prime instigator of the 1832 Battle of Velasco, the incident that sparked the revolt against Mexico. After Texas won its independence, Waller was a signer of the Texas Declaration of Independence, represented several communities during the provisional stages of early Texas government, and served as a delegate from Brazoria for the Convention of 1836.

SIGNER OF THE TEXAS DECLARATION OF INDEPENDENCE · LAID OUT THE CITY OF AUSTIN AND WAS ITS FIRST MAYOR · · WALLER COUNTY WAS NAMED IN HIS HONOR

Edwin Waller, signer of the Texas Declaration of Independence, died in 1881 and was buried at a family cemetery in Waller County before his remains were interred at the Texas State Cemetery in 1928. PICB 10971, Austin History Center, Austin Public Library.

He quickly realized that building a city could bring battles of another kind. Once Waterloo's name was changed and its selection as capital of the Republic was finalized, Waller pushed ahead with the construction of government buildings and employee housing and the establishment of a street system. By October 1839, President Lamar and the majority of his cabinet moved to Austin, and Waller was elected the first mayor, although he only served for a short time.

He came face to face with trouble when President Mirabeau B. Lamar nominated him to be postmaster general of the Republic. Waller's nomination ran into opposition from Houston. Lamar and Houston were bitter political enemies and seemed instinctively to hold opposing viewpoints on almost any issue. Predictably, Houston took exception to the Waller nomination and tried to block it. In a move designed to tarnish Waller's reputation, Albert C. Horton, Houston's faithful supporter, publicly questioned items in Waller's contract for building the new Capitol.

Personally offended, Waller attacked Horton on the grounds of the Capitol. Inside, members of Congress recessed to watch the two distinguished gentlemen slug it out while a mob of citizens gathered to view the spectacle. Waller and Horton had to be separated, as onlookers jumped into the fray in defense of their mayor.

Waller won the larger battle, too: he received the nomination for postmaster general, thanks to a tie-breaking vote by Anson Jones, president of the Senate. Waller served a short time as postmaster general. He resigned to fight at the Battle of Plum Creek in 1840, and then returned to a quieter life as a farmer in Austin County, where he was also a judge. In 1861, he participated in the Secession Convention. He was the only signer of the Texas Declaration of Independence to sign the ordinance of secession.

Edwin Waller died January 3, 1881, and was buried in Waller County at a family cemetery. His remains, and those of his wife, were brought to their final resting place at the Texas State Cemetery in 1928.

THOMAS WILLIAM WARD

1807–1872

REPUBLIC HILL, SECTION 1 (C1), ROW N, PLOT 10

Thomas William Ward, also known as "Peg Leg" Ward, was interred at the Texas State Cemetery in honor of his political and military contributions to Republic-era Texas and early statehood. As his moniker suggests, Peg Leg bore the scars of battle. Ward lost a leg in an early battle in Texas's war for independence against Mexico. Years later, at a celebration marking the fifth anniversary of Texas independence, an errant cannonball tore through Ward's body, destroying an eye and an arm.

Ward was born in Ireland in 1807 to an English immigrant and his wife. The elder Ward was a landowner and claimed to be descended from the Barons Ward, a title that was created in 1644.

At the age of fifteen, the younger Ward enrolled in the military academy of the British East India Company, which had a monopoly on all trade in the East Indies. Ward, however, took a greater interest in improving his own homeland, and after a few years in the academy, he trained in architecture. Apparently showing a talent in the field, Ward was "entrusted with the direction and construction of important erections in Dublin," according to a biographical essay by Ward McCampbell housed at the Austin History Center.

Ward left for Quebec in 1828 and shortly after ventured south to New Orleans, where he gained some prominence as an engineer and architect and where his role in Texas history began. He joined the New Orleans Greys, two military companies of US volunteers that fought in the Texas War for Independence from Mexico. They arrived in Texas in time to participate in the Siege of Bexar, which lasted from October to December 1835.

The Siege of Bexar proved fateful for Ward. On December 7, during the culminating battle of the siege, Ward, at the head of an artillery company, followed Colonel Benjamin R. Milam into San Antonio. During the battle there, Ward lost his leg to a cannonball, and Milam was killed by a sniper's bullet to the head. Legend has it that Milam's body and Ward's leg are buried in the same grave. On December 9, the siege was broken. Mexican forces surrendered and retreated south from Texas.

Wounded and honorably discharged from the army, Ward returned to New Orleans where he was fitted with a wooden leg. He raised another regiment of men and marched to Texas. The volunteers arrived a month too late, however, as the revolution ended at San Jacinto in April 1836. Nonetheless, in May, interim president David G. Burnet commissioned Ward a colonel in the Texas Army, and he served under General Thomas J. Rusk. Eventually, he settled in the newly founded city of Houston.

With his days as a revolutionary at an end, Ward once again turned to architecture. On February 18, 1837, Augustus C. Allen, one of the founders of Houston, granted Ward the contract to build the Texas Capitol there. The goal was to complete the building in time for the first Congressional meeting, but building materials arrived too late. Ward completed the building in time for the Second Session of the First Congress. He served as a member of the Harrisburg County's Board of Land Commissioners in 1838.

Thomas William Ward, known widely as "Peg Leg" Ward, was interred at the Texas State Cemetery in 1872. Used with the permission of Texas State Library and Archives Commission, Archives and Information Services Division, 1997/1-36-3.

The presence of the Capitol in Houston notwithstanding, Texas President Mirabeau B. Lamar moved the capital to Waterloo in the summer of 1839. Ward followed his project to the city renamed in honor of Stephen F. Austin. There he immersed himself in the effort to build a new capital city. He served as the chief clerk for the House of Representatives during the Fourth Congress and was elected mayor of Austin in the fall of 1840 after the first mayor, Edwin Waller, resigned to work on plans to design the new city. During his brief tenure in that office, Ward created eight districts with a representative from each serving on the city council. He also coordinated the sale of town lots.

Because of his knowledge of land law, Ward was appointed the commissioner of the General Land Office in 1841 by newly elected President Sam Houston. He served as commissioner for seven years. Land laws in the new republic were complex and unclear, and surveys—oftentimes conducted by untrained surveyors—were inconsistent, if not downright conflicting. Ward labored to make sense of them. He also confronted rampant fraud and disreputable land speculators by establishing a system that is still in operation today.

Even though the revolution was over, life proved dangerous for Ward. On March 2, 1841, he met disaster while loading an artillery piece that was to be used in celebrating the fifth anniversary of Texas Independence Day. The cannon accidentally discharged, and the ball ripped into the former soldier. His right arm was destroyed, and, according to Noah Smithwick's book, *The Evolution of a State, or, Recollections of Old Texas Days*, his right eye was severely damaged.

Ward recovered, though, and continued to serve Texas—most dramatically in the Archive War. In 1842, President Sam Houston ordered the relocation of the state archives from Austin to Houston. The order was a preventive measure in response to the perceived threat of attack from Mexicans, who had just besieged San Antonio. Austinites feared that removal of the archives would spell the end to the city as capital of Texas. A contingent of angry citizens confronted the Texas Rangers, who were sent to escort the archives to a safer location. Ward was among those in the Rangers contingent fired upon by innkeeper Angelina Eberly, who fired the town cannon to alert the citizenry to the removal. The Rangers surrendered the archives to the vigilantes and the archives remained in Austin.

Ward's role in the Archive War likely led to his only political defeat. After Texas joined the United States on February 19, 1846, Ward was forced to stand for election as General Land Office commissioner, a position to which he had been appointed when Texas was a republic. His opponent was George Washington Smyth, a signer of the Texas Declaration of Independence. Ward was defeated, probably because his loyalty to Austin was still in question. However, Austin voters reelected him mayor in 1853.

He did not hold the position for long. Ward resigned as mayor in September 1853 to accept an appointment by President Franklin Pierce to serve as US consul to Panama. In ailing health, Ward returned to the United States in 1857 and vigorously campaigned against secession in the election of 1860. After the Civil War, Ward again served as mayor of Austin when Provisional Governor Andrew J. Hamilton appointed him to the position in 1865. In October of the same year, he left Austin to serve as President Andrew Johnson's appointee as Corpus Christi's customs collector, a position he held until 1869 when President Ulysses S. Grant fired him.

On November 26, 1872, the *Daily Democratic Statesman* reported Ward's death from typhoid fever, and he was laid to rest in Austin at the Texas State Cemetery, under the auspices of the Masons and the Odd Fellows. In honor of his service for and to the Republic and State of Texas, Governor Edmund J. Davis issued a proclamation closing State offices and ordered the flag at the Capitol to be lowered to half-staff in honor of "this brave old hero."

A replacement headstone of pink Texas granite was erected on Ward's grave in 1932 by the State of Texas during an upsurge of interest in the State Cemetery.

ROBERT POTTER

1799–1842

REPUBLIC HILL, SECTION 2 (C2), ROW U, PLOT 5

Robert Potter, called the founder of the Texas Navy, was not a man to be easily classified. While he did much good, he had a severe temper and his life was marked by bouts of extreme violence. He was born in June of 1799, in Granville County, North Carolina, and as a boy idolized the American naval hero John Paul Jones. At the age of sixteen, Potter left home to join the United States Navy.

Potter was ambitious, there is no doubt. By the age of twenty-one, he became frustrated with the direction of his naval career; he left the Navy and decided to study law. He was elected to the United States Congress in 1829 and then the North Carolina Legislature.

It was while serving in Congress that Potter's violent temper gained public attention. The congressman suspected his wife of carrying on an affair with two unlikely candidates—her cousins, a minister and a seventeen-year-old boy. He confronted the minister and words were exchanged. Potter beat, hog-tied, and then castrated him. The unfortunate youth suffered the same fate. Potter returned home, where his wife, perhaps in fear for her own life, confessed to adultery. He was jailed, tried, and convicted for the assaults. But the sentence was light: six months in jail and a fine of one thousand dollars. Personally, though, Potter's losses were great. He gave up his position in Congress, and a few years later, his wife divorced him. She died not long afterward, and her death was followed by that of their only daughter. A son, the sole surviving child, was declared "mentally incompetent."

Despite evidence of past hotheadedness, Potter was again elected to the North Carolina Legislature, but was removed from office for cheating at cards with his fellow legislators. It is more likely that the real reason behind his removal from office were the crimes against his wife's cousins.

His career in shambles, Potter left for New Orleans and traveled to Texas, a hotbed of political activity at the time, and Potter loved politics as much as a good fight. By 1835, Texas was in the midst of preparations for independence from Mexico, and Potter's political experience in North Carolina proved to be a valuable asset to the new republic. He was elected a delegate to the Convention of 1836, signed the Texas Declaration of Independence, and helped write the Constitution of the Republic of Texas.

Potter's actual involvement in the Naval Department is debatable. He held the title Secretary of the Navy, but some historians believe he accomplished little in the position. Regardless, by October 1836 Potter was no longer Secretary of the Texas Navy.

But, there was always politics, and once again Potter entered the political arena, this time as a Republic of Texas senator in 1840. Potter used his position to champion the Navy and discovered himself running counter to other elected officials—in particular, President Sam Houston. Houston was skeptical of the Navy for the questionable administration, but also maintained a long-standing feud with Potter over their elections to the Convention of 1836, when Potter defeated Houston and many others vying for a delegate's position.

Robert Potter, signer of the Texas
Declaration of Independence
and veteran of the Battle of San
Jacinto, was interred at the Texas
State Cemetery in 1928. Used with
the permission of Texas State
Library and Archives Commission,
Archives and Information Services
Division, 1934/13-11.

Potter had other, more destructive, enemies as well. At the conclusion of the Sixth Congress of the Republic of Texas, the senator journeyed home to Potter's Point on Caddo Lake. Along the way, he decided to settle a score with one of his enemies, William Rose. Rose was reputedly a leader on the Regulator side of the Regulator-Moderator War, an East Texas feud revolving around land deals and swindles. Potter assembled a band of Rose opponents and set off to arrest him. Unable to locate Rose, the band disassembled and Potter returned to his home. On the evening of March 2, 1842, Rose gathered his allies, headed for Potter's Point, and surrounded Potter's house. Potter escaped and ran to the lake, which he then tried to swim across. When he came up for air, he was shot in the head.

Rose and his band were taken to jail, but the case was later dismissed for lack of evidence, despite the eyewitness testimony of Potter's wife. Potter's body was later recovered from the lake and buried at Potter's Point. In 1928, his remains were laid to rest in the Texas State Cemetery.

REPUBLIC OF TEXAS

JOSIAH PUGH WILBARGER

1801–1845

REPUBLIC HILL, SECTION 1 (C1), ROW T, PLOT 7

Josiah Pugh Wilbarger was an early Texas settler and veteran of the Texas War for Independence. But he holds a unique place in Texas history for other, more colorful, reasons. Wilbarger had the misfortune to be attacked by an Indian raiding party in 1833. Two in the party of five were killed, but Wilbarger—shot once with a bullet, once with an arrow, and then scalped—survived.

Although the scalping story has become legend, Wilbarger was certainly a real person. Some sources claim he was born in Bourbon County, Kentucky, but others say he was born in Rockingham County, Virginia, and moved to Kentucky in 1818. Wilbarger then relocated to Pike County, Missouri, in 1823 and married Margaret Barker in September 1827. They left for Texas soon after their wedding, arriving at Matagorda on December 26 the same year.

Wilbarger taught school at Matagorda for about a year before moving to La Grange. There, he taught and worked as a surveyor until he settled in Stephen F. Austin's Little Colony in a bend of the Colorado River near present-day Bastrop. He was granted a league of land in January 1832—many sources hold that Wilbarger was the first Texas colonist to settle in the area.

The story of Josiah Wilbarger was a campfire tale well before University of Texas professor and author J. Frank Dobie and others wrote it down for popular consumption. It was also turned into an episode of the television series *Death Valley Days* in 1966. Dobie's version is that Wilbarger and four other men left their holdings to scout for land. While eating lunch at

nearby Walnut Spring, the group was caught off guard by a group of Indians. According to some accounts, the attackers were from the Comanche tribe; others say the raiding party was from the Kickapoo tribe.

Two men died, two escaped, and Wilbarger was left for dead. The two survivors fled to the house of Reuben Hornsby, a fellow settler in the area, where they reported that three of their companions had been killed. A rider was sent down the Colorado River for aid, only to discover a survivor among the dead. It was Wilbarger, who had been scalped and also suffered additional wounds in the neck and leg. Wilbarger claimed to have been conscious when the attackers sliced off his scalp.

And then the legend takes a more mythical turn. Reuben Hornsby's wife had not believed Wilbarger's surviving companions' report of his death. Dobie wrote, "About midnight Sarah Hornsby, a remarkably plucky and resolute woman, roused her husband saying, 'Wilbarger is not dead. I saw him in a dream. He sits under a large post oak tree, naked, scalped and covered with blood.'"[3] She succeeded in convincing her husband and the two survivors to set out in search of their abandoned friend. They agreed to go, but waited for reinforcements to arrive the next day from colonies farther south.

At Walnut Spring, Wilbarger lasted through the night, gathering enough strength to drag himself to a nearby watering hole to drink and bathe his wounds. He survived by eating snails during the day and into the next night. As each hour ticked by, the wounds festered—Wilbarger later recounted that he felt blowflies

A period sketch by T. J. Owen of the scalping of Josiah Wilbarger. Wilbarger, a Texas colonist and veteran of the Texas War of Independence, is known in Texas legend as "the man who wouldn't die." Used with the permission of Texas State Library and Archives Commission, Archives and Information Services Division, 1998/1-11-3. Photograph was taken from a sketch titled "Scalping of Josiah Wilbarger" in J. W. Wilbarger's Indian Depredations in Texas, 1890.

SCALPING OF JOSIAH WILBARGER.

laying their eggs in his scalp wounds and could sense the maggots hatching in his skin.

By this time Wilbarger was desperate. He decided to crawl to the Hornsby house, but only made it about three-quarters of a mile before collapsing under an oak tree. Probably delirious, Wilbarger always claimed that he then saw the figure of his sister, Margaret Clifton. Dobie wrote, "Standing near him, the sister said, her voice calm and restful, 'Brother Josiah, you are too weak to go any farther by yourself. Remain here under this tree and friends will come take care of you before the setting of another sun.'"[4]

As Wilbarger lay near death under the oak, Sarah Hornsby worked on his behalf elsewhere. She told her husband and the other rescuers to take three sheets with them: two for burying the dead men and the other to wrap around Wilbarger. Late the next day, the men found Wilbarger, soaked in blood and naked except for a single sock on one foot. They carried him back to the Hornsby house where they treated him with poultices and oils.

Dobie asserted that after Wilbarger and Sarah Hornsby compared their separate visions, they determined that the insistent female in Hornsby's dream appeared to her shortly after Margaret Clifton's spectral visit to her brother. In a popular twist to this tale, Wilbarger later learned the fate of his sister Margaret.

Dobie wrote, "It was not until many weeks had passed that he learned she had died the day before he was wounded and even at the hour of his vision was spending her first night in the grave."[5]

Wilbarger lived an active life after his brush with death. The wounds to his throat and to his leg healed completely, but the skin over his skull never completely healed. To hide the exposed wound, his wife sewed a special cap, which he supposedly always wore.

Eventually, though, the scalping indirectly resulted in his death. Dobie, among other tale spinners, claimed that Wilbarger, who was working in a mill on his ranch, died instantly when he hit his head on a beam on April 11, 1845. He was buried in Fairview Cemetery near his home.

The Wilbarger legend lived on and soon merged with the stories of other legendary Texans. William A. A. "Bigfoot" Wallace, the Texas Ranger and frontiersman, recounted a story of meeting Wilbarger near La Grange one night in 1838. According to the story, Wallace was eating dinner with friends around a campfire when Wilbarger walked into the ring of light to warm his head. Wallace purportedly asked Wilbarger what was wrong with his head and Wilbarger responded, "I've been scalped by the Indians."

Wilbarger and his son John were interred under a pink Texas granite marker in the Texas State Cemetery in 1932.

JOEL WALTER ROBISON

1815–1889

AND

JAMES AUSTIN SYLVESTER

1807–1882

REPUBLIC HILL, SECTION 1 (C1), ROW P, PLOTS 4 AND 5

By all accounts, Joel Robison and James Sylvester were distinguished soldiers during the fight for Texas independence, but their claim to fame hinges on their involvement in the capture of the defeated Mexican general, Santa Anna. Their accounts of the apprehension differ, but the outcome for the vanquished Mexican army was the same.

The Battle of San Jacinto was the decisive battle of the war for independence and a devastating defeat for a far superior Mexican army. The Texas army, led by General Sam Houston, surprised Santa Anna's troops on April 21, 1836, and in a short eighteen minutes killed more than six hundred Mexican soldiers, wounded two hundred, and took seven hundred prisoners. Texas casualties were comparatively light—nine deaths and thirty wounded. At the end of the battle, Santa Anna had fled.

The next morning, General Houston ordered a search for General Santa Anna and other errant Mexican soldiers. Several detachments were ordered to conduct the search. The detachment, led by Captain James Sylvester, was composed of Joel Robison, Joseph D. Vermillion, Alfred H. Miles, David Cole, and Sion Bostick.

There are inconsistencies in the accounts of the capture of Santa Anna. Captain Sylvester's version differs from that of future Texas House member Joel Robison. Sylvester claimed his detachment went off in search of food, while he—by himself—happened to stumble across a Mexican soldier. Sylvester noticed the high quality of the soldier's shirt and became suspicious. After further interrogation, the captive claimed to be an aide to General Santa Anna.

It was at this point, according to Sylvester, that members of his detachment rejoined him. In his account, there is no mention of Robison being present, but a revision to the account of Santa Anna's capture was later recorded on his headstone: he "erroneously referred to Robison as Thompson."

Sylvester and the others (presumably including Robison) headed back to the camp. Their captive somewhat brazenly complained of fatigue and asked to ride, refusing to relinquish the horse until he was finally ordered to dismount. The reason for his mystifying arrogance became clear once the party reached camp, where the captives greeted the detachment and their charge with a loud chorus of "El Presidente!"

According to Robison, however, the entire search party came upon the mysterious soldier. It was Robison—the only one of the detachment who could speak Spanish—who interrogated the prisoner. As to the trip

back to camp, there seems to be slight variation: Robison claimed to feel sorry for the prisoner, who was threatened with death by another member of the detachment, and gave him his horse to ride. Both Sylvester and Robison agree on one thing—that the Mexican prisoners unwittingly exposed the identity of their leader when he was escorted into the Texan camp.

James Austin Sylvester was born in Baltimore, Maryland, in 1807. His family moved to Kentucky and, when he was old enough, he moved to work at the *Cincinnati Enquirer*. But by 1835 word had spread around the country about the Texas fight for independence, and Sylvester, along with fifty other men, joined a company of Kentucky riflemen. The regiment, led by Sidney Sherman, arrived in Texas in early 1836 and Sylvester was immediately commissioned a captain in the Texas reserves. Following the fall of the Alamo, he joined General Sam Houston in Gonzales and they proceeded to march on San Jacinto.

Joel Walter Robison was born in October 1815 in Washington County, Georgia. At the age of sixteen, Robison and his family moved to Texas and settled near Columbia. His participation in the fight for Texas independence began at the beginning, the Battle of Velasco in 1832. Robison also participated in the Siege of Bexar, the Grass Fight, and the Battle of Concepción, all in 1835. In addition, it is generally believed Robison

was Colonel William B. Travis's last messenger from the Alamo. He eventually joined up with Colonel Edward Burleson's First Regiment, Texas Volunteers, at the Battle of San Jacinto.

Sylvester's and Robison's paths crossed once and only once—the day after the Battle of San Jacinto, when they were part of the party to capture Santa Anna. In 1842, Sylvester joined the Somervell Expedition, charged with punishing the Mexican army for its continuing raids into Texas. The next year, Sylvester left Texas and resumed his journalism career with the *New Orleans Picayune*, where he was employed until his death on April 9, 1882.

Robison, on the other hand, stayed in Texas. Following the Battle of San Jacinto, he served in the Texas Rangers. By 1840, he was a successful farmer and public servant. In 1860, the United States was on the verge of civil war, and Robison was elected to the Texas House of Representatives. He only served one term and voted in favor of secession. Robison's last public service was as a representative to the Constitutional Convention of 1875. He died on August 4, 1889.

Sylvester was buried in the Odd Fellows Rest Cemetery in New Orleans. His remains were laid to rest in the Texas State Cemetery in 1937.

Robison was buried next to his wife in the Florida Chapel Cemetery in Round Top, and their remains were moved to the Texas State Cemetery in 1932.

THE CAPTORS OF SANTA ANNA WERE
JAMES A. SYLVESTER, JOEL WALTER ROBISON,
JOSEPH D. VERMILLION, ALFRED H. MILES, DAVID COLE

JOANNA TROUTMAN

1818–1879

Because she sewed one of the first Lone Star flags flown in Texas, Joanna Troutman is widely considered the "Betsy Ross of Texas." Despite her inspiring contribution to the state, though, it took a special gubernatorial order by O. B. Colquitt in 1913 to inter Troutman, a Georgia native, in the State Cemetery.

On February 13, 1913, the Texas Legislature bestowed on Troutman official recognition as the sole creator of the first Texas flag. Some controversy still exists—regardless of the legislature's pronouncement—because other flags bearing the Lone Star flew over Texas even before Troutman's flag. For example, the so-called Long flag was carried by James Long, the leader of an early attempt by Anglo-Americans to wrest Texas from Spain. Long was captured and imprisoned in Mexico City, where he was eventually executed. Nevertheless, Troutman's flag, which was destroyed during the Goliad Massacre in 1836, remains the most emblematic of the state's struggle for independence.

Joanna Troutman was born in Crawford County, Georgia, on February 19, 1818, the daughter of Hiram Baldwin Troutman and Balsora N. Ellis. The Troutmans owned a plantation and an inn, named the Troutman Inn.

In 1835, public sentiment in the United States was running high in favor of the Anglo-American settlers fighting for an independent Texas. Citizens rallied across the South to send men and money to Texas to aid in the fight. One of the most persuasive supporters was Hugh McCleod, a spirited speaker who fired up a town meeting in Macon, Georgia, by announcing that he would resign his current commission in the Third United States Infantry to volunteer for the Texas cause. He urged other men to do the same.

Twelve days after that town meeting, three companies from Macon and two from Columbus were assembled and equipped. Led by Colonel William Ward, they marched across Georgia, stopping along the way at Knoxville, where the Troutman Inn was located.

The fight for independence in Texas fired the imaginations of many people in the United States, and Joanna Troutman was among those who eagerly followed accounts of the revolution. To show her support, she decided to sew a flag for the Georgian volunteers marching west. In mid-November 1835, Troutman presented her flag to Colonel Ward on the steps of the Troutman Inn.

The companies headed west, trekking on to Texas. The Georgian troops first unfurled their banner at the American Hotel in Velasco on January 8, 1836. The flag eventually reached Goliad, where Colonel James W. Fannin, a fellow Georgian, flew it over the fort on March 8, 1836, to celebrate recent news of the signing of the Texas Declaration of Independence six days earlier.

The Troutman flag, also known as the "Liberty or Death" flag, was a two-sided white silk banner. At the center on one side was a blue five-pointed star with the words "Liberty or Death" painted below; on the other side was another blue five-pointed star with the Latin motto, "*Ubi Libertas Habitat, Ibi Nostra Patria Est*" ("where liberty resides, there is our homeland") painted underneath.

Unfortunately, nothing of the flag remains today. Only its remnants, tattered by weather, flew above the Battle of Coleto on March 19, 1836, the final battle of the Goliad Campaign. The Texans who survived that onslaught were imprisoned by the Mexican army at Goliad and subsequently executed by order of General Antonio López de Santa Anna on March 27, 1836, in what came to be known as the Goliad Massacre. Troutman's flag was likely burned with the bodies of the Texan dead.

Troutman probably did not expect anything in return for making her flag, but Texas General Memucan Hunt saw fit to present her with a gift of silver in gratitude. The silver—massive quantities of spoons and forks—was booty obtained by General Thomas Jefferson Rusk at the Battle of San Jacinto. He passed the silver on to Hunt to give to Troutman. No other documentation indicates that anyone else who sewed a flag for the Texas cause received any of that silver—not even Sarah Dodson, a Texan who sewed a flag for the Texan Harrisburg Company in September 1835.

Troutman married S. L. Pope in 1839, and the couple moved to Elmwood, a prosperous plantation near Knoxville, in 1840. They had four sons. Her husband died in 1872, and she married W. G. Vinson, a Georgia state legislator, in 1875. She died on July 23, 1879, at Elmwood and was buried next to her first husband.

In 1913, Texas Governor O. B. Colquitt secured permission to have Joanna Troutman's remains brought to Texas for interment in the State Cemetery in Austin. A bronze statue by Pompeo L. Coppini stands atop a gray, granite marker with a plaque stating: "Gentle, pure, patriotic, the hands of Joanna Troutman wrought her love of liberty into the beautiful lone star flag which witnessed the sacrifice of the men who brought it to Texas as the emblem of independence." Additionally, there are three bronze plaques honoring the names of all those individuals who died at Goliad.

A Texas flag flies at the top of Monument Hill, in the northeast portion of the Texas State Cemetery. Numerous Texas flags fly over the Cemetery, including a 30-foot-by-50-foot flag that can be seen from the Capitol. Photograph by Laurence Parent.

Grave of Joanna Troutman, called the "Betsy Ross of Texas" for sewing one of the first Texas flags featuring a lone star. The bronze statue atop her monument was created by Pompeo Coppini. Photograph by Laurence Parent.

CHAPTER THREE

CIVIL WAR

*

AND

*

RECONSTRUCTION

INTRODUCTION BY GENERAL HAL HORNBURG

INTRODUCTION

BY GENERAL HAL HORNBURG

Hal Hornburg is a retired four-star general, United States Air Force. Before his retirement, he was commander, Air Combat Command, Langley Air Force Base, Langley, Virginia. General Hornburg is a native Texan and graduated from Texas A&M University in 1968.

I served in the United States Air Force for more than thirty-six years. I saw combat action in three areas during three eras: Vietnam as a lieutenant, Desert Storm as a colonel, and air operations over Bosnia as a two-star general.

I'm a Texan. When I hugged and kissed my young wife good-bye and left Dallas for Vietnam, it was one of the most difficult days of my life. I didn't know if I'd ever see her again, but good luck and great training brought me home, and we picked up where we left off. In July 1970, when I returned to Vietnam from our Rest and Recuperation (R&R), I learned that my best friend had not returned from a mission. He's listed on The Wall (Vietnam Veterans Memorial) in Washington, and his status remains missing in action; his bodily remains may never be found. A marker at the United States Air Force Academy commemorates his life.

I think of the times I went to war. The first was for a year, the next for seven and a half months . . . the third was, due to technology, fought from a NATO base in Italy. With all this offered as perspective, I think of those who marched off to the unknown during the Civil War. Some rest here—others could not come home.

They were mostly young. They believed in their cause. They were committed. Some looked at their

FRED CARLETON
BORN—LONDON, ENGLAND—APRIL 15, 1841
DIED—AUSTIN, TEXAS—NOVEMBER 11, 1910
MEMBER CO.C 16th REGIMENT TEXAS VOLUNTEER INFANTRY C.S.A.
ONE OF THE FOUNDERS OF CONFEDERATE HOME, AUSTIN, TEXAS
ONE OF THE ORGANIZERS W. AND O. HOME I.O.O.F.
CORSICANA, TEXAS
GRAND SIRE I.O.O.F. 1896—1898

Erected by the Odd Fellows of Texas.

FATHER   MOTHER

KYSER

Confederate Field at sunrise. Many of the Confederates buried at the Cemetery did not die during the Civil War, but rather perished of natural causes in Austin after living at the Confederate Men's Home in the capital city. Photograph by Laurence Parent.

Confederate Field at the Texas State Cemetery is the final resting place of more than 2,000 Confederate veterans and their widows. Photograph by Laurence Parent.

mothers' tears as they prepared to leave. Others hugged their wives; others, their wives and children. Some then mounted up, while others simply turned their backs on all they loved and started putting one foot in front of the other. Some looked back in dread, others in peace, some just kept walking. To look back might cause them to lose their courage, and that just wouldn't do at all.

There were no planes, no buses, no trains—no easy way to get these men to their first battle. And when they fought, they were a long way from home, in places like Tennessee, Mississippi, and Virginia. Hot places, cold places, bone dry, and soaking wet. Few, if any, letters from home. Letters were written, but, chances were, they'd never be delivered and, if they were, the news would be months old. Day after day led to month after month. They were lonely and, after a while, they forgot what they were fighting for, so they fought for each other. That's what soldiers do.

These were farmers, ranchers, mule skinners, music teachers, dry goods salesmen. It didn't matter. The call came. Texans answered. They went, they served. Some died and were buried where they fell. Others, somehow, made it home. They lie here today among their comrades. Here in this beautiful place, in this sacred ground. Come stand here and be a part of the silence. Be proud of them and of their courage. Don't weep, but find joy in the fact that they were Texans and Americans who willingly did their duty. All gave some, but some gave all. Of a soldier, nothing more can be asked. Say a prayer for them and let it remind you to also say one for the men and women who drape themselves in the cloth of service to their nation, even today.

★

Grave of Francis Richard Lubbock and wife, Adele F. Baron Lubbock. Lubbock was governor of Texas during the Civil War and was an aide-de-camp to Jefferson Davis. Photograph by Will Erwin.

The final resting place of General Albert Sidney Johnston, commander of the Army of the Mississippi for the Confederate States of America during the Civil War. Photograph by Laurence Parent.

SHILOH
CHARLES S DYER
REST WITH OVER
2500 CONFEDERATE
SOLDIERS
WHOSE BURIAL SITE
REMAINS KNOWN
ONLY TO GOD

G. W. RO
DI
FEB. 6
AGED 6

Examples of Confederate headstones at the Texas State Cemetery. Though Confederate Field looks uniform from afar, there is quite a bit of variety among the Confederate headstones, from lettering style to material to size. Photographs by Will Erwin.

The grave of Antonio Briones, US Army private during the Civil War. Briones is one of only a few Union soldiers buried in the Texas State Cemetery. Photograph by Laurence Parent

The central issue of the Civil War was states' rights, with slavery the underlying issue. The Civil War divided the United States like no other event in our history. Texas played a major role, both politically and militarily. Buried at the Cemetery are individuals who participated in the Civil War for both the Confederacy and the Union. Generals, politicians, and common soldiers represent both the Union and Confederate causes.

★

ALBERT SIDNEY JOHNSTON

1803–1862

CONFEDERATE FIELD, SECTION 2, ROW A, PLOT 13

Albert Sidney Johnston fought in three armies during his lifetime: the United States Army, the Republic of Texas Army, and the Confederate States Army. He loved his adopted state, claiming, "When I die, I want a handful of Texas soil on my breast."[1]

Throughout his military career, he was known as an honest, dignified leader and was respected as a soldier. General P. G. T. Beauregard described Johnston as a "great and good man, who many believe that, if he had been at the head of our Confederate Government during the late war, the latter might have ended differently, if not with success to us, certainly with less disastrous consequences."[2]

Johnston was born February 2, 1803, in Washington, Kentucky. He came from a distinguished New England family that had migrated to Kentucky in the 1780s. Johnston entered Transylvania University in nearby Lexington, but after two years he sought an appointment to the United States Military Academy. He entered West Point in 1822 and following graduation was assigned to a post on Lake Ontario.

By 1832, the year the Black Hawk War broke out, he was sent to the Sixth Regiment as adjutant. The Black Hawk War was not a major conflict, but Johnston distinguished himself and attracted the attention of his superiors. One general wrote, "He has talents of the first order, a gallant soldier by profession and education."[3]

Johnston's military career was marked with periods of retirement to private life. Family concerns led him to resign his commission in the United States Army in 1834. During this chapter in his life, his father, brother, infant child, and wife would all die. Perhaps because of these tragedies, he went to Texas to fight for the Republic of Texas Army in July 1836. He joined as an enlisted man, but talent and training eventually led to promotion. His career advanced quickly and by September 1836, Johnston was named the adjutant general of the Republic, with the rank of colonel in the regular army. Shortly thereafter, he was appointed senior brigadier general of the Republic of Texas Army.

Some colleagues, most notably Felix Huston, resented Johnston's meteoric ascent. Huston had been appointed junior brigadier general and temporary commander by

Albert Sidney Johnston,
Confederate general and commander
of the Republic of Texas Army,
died at the Battle of Shiloh in 1862
and was buried in New Orleans
before being interred at the Texas
State Cemetery in 1867. Johnston's
monument was designed and
constructed by internationally
renowned sculptor Elisabet Ney.
Courtesy of the Daughters of the
Republic of Texas.

President Sam Houston. He took offense at Johnston's appointment as commander and challenged Johnston to a duel. On the morning of February 5, 1837, the two men met and faced each other with pistols. Both parties fired and missed, and finally Huston managed to shoot Johnston through his right hip. Although the wound wasn't fatal, it left Johnston partially paralyzed and he walked with a limp for the rest of his life.

Huston came to regret the incident and reconciled himself to Johnston's seniority. After a long recovery, Johnston took command of the army in 1837. He resigned, however, after he lost confidence in the Houston administration over the handling of military affairs with Mexico and the Indian population. Houston had disbanded much of the army and the Mexican military began making raids across the Rio Grande. There is also some evidence to suggest that Houston turned on Johnston, causing a rift.

A view of the iconic grave of Albert Sidney Johnston from Confederate Field. Johnston was commander of the Army of the Mississippi during the Civil War and many of the Confederate veterans buried at the Cemetery would have been under his command. The white headstones denote the graves of Confederate enlisted men and face Johnston's monument. Photograph by Laurence Parent.

The rift widened in 1838 when Mirabeau Lamar was elected president of the Republic of Texas. He selected Johnston to be secretary of war, a position that, at the time, was focused mostly on problems with the Comanche, who had made raids on the new capital city of Austin. In March 1840, Johnston resigned his position as secretary of war. He sold his property in Kentucky and Missouri and bought land in Austin and Galveston. He focused on his personal life, developing an interest in land speculation. He also remarried; his bride was Eliza Griffin of Kentucky.

Following Texas's annexation, Johnston was being touted as the colonel of a new United States regiment stationed in Texas in 1845. Despite several recommendations from prominent military officials, including General Zachary Taylor, Johnston's appointment was opposed by newly elected United States Senator Sam Houston. Houston blocked the 1845 appointment, but was not able to stop the men of the First Texas Infantry Regiment from electing Johnston as their colonel during the Mexican-American War in 1846.

General Taylor subsequently appointed Johnston to be inspector general to the staff of Major William O. Butler, commander of the division of volunteers. Following the Battle of Monterrey during the Mexican-American War, Johnston's enlistment was up, and he returned to Galveston to enjoy civilian life with his wife.

By March 1855, Johnston was called back into military service, this time as a colonel in the Second United States Cavalry. The regiment's primary mission was to guard Texas and the western frontier against the Indians, particularly the Comanche. However, the Second Cavalry was later to play a pivotal role in the Civil War. In 1855, Robert E. Lee was second in command; William J. Hardee, E. Kirby Smith, and John Bell Hood also served as officers. In 1857, Johnston was asked to lead an expedition to Utah to quell the Mormon rebellion. His conduct in Utah brought him to the attention of many power brokers in the Democratic Party, and his name came up as a possible presidential candidate.

Johnston was appointed commander of the Department of the Pacific in 1861. He and his family moved to San Francisco, but the appointment was short-lived:

Texas seceded from the Union and Johnston resigned his commission.

He then journeyed to the South to visit his longtime friend and classmate Jefferson Davis. Davis was assembling troops and made Johnston a general in the Confederate States Army. His command stretched from Kentucky to Louisiana.

Johnston achieved one of the great successes of the war: the April 6, 1862, pre-dawn attack on General William T. Sherman's Union troops at Shiloh. Johnston's decision to attack caught Sherman off guard because General Ulysses S. Grant was nine miles away and Sherman did not expect an attack. Many historians have called the 5 a.m. attack one of the great strategic surprises of the war.

The Battle of Shiloh was to be Johnston's last. Throughout the morning, Confederate forces bombarded the Federal position. Even in the heat of battle, Johnston never lost his sense of humanity. He ordered the Confederate doctors and surgeons to assist the Union soldiers in need of care, commenting, "They were our enemies a moment ago. They are prisoners now." He made no exceptions—even his personal surgeon was instructed to care for the Union wounded.

But by 2 p.m., the Confederate forces were showing signs of exhaustion. In an effort to rally his troops, Johnston rode to the front of the line and revived his men with a rousing speech. Yelling, "I will lead you," he swung his horse out into the field and immediately came under a barrage of friendly and enemy fire. Johnston was hit and fell in his saddle. He was taken to safety but died from loss of blood.

His body was taken to New Orleans for temporary interment in St. Louis Cemetery. But Johnston loved Texas and had made it clear he wanted to be buried there. So in 1867, the Texas Legislature moved his remains to the Texas State Cemetery. Despite the disapproval of federal authorities, thousands of mourners lined the streets from Houston to Austin to pay their respects.

In 1903, the Texas Legislature commissioned Austin sculptor Elisabet Ney to design a statue and a Gothic-style wrought iron structure for Johnston's grave.

FRANCIS RICHARD LUBBOCK

1815–1905

REPUBLIC HILL, SECTION 1 (C1), ROW G, PLOT 19

Francis Richard Lubbock, buried on Republic Hill beneath a sculpture of a cloth-draped cross, was present at the very end of the Civil War, when Confederate President Jefferson Davis was taken into Federal custody.

Lubbock was with Davis as the Confederacy fell, and they attempted to flee from Virginia to Texas. Both were captured at Irwinville, Georgia, along with Davis's family on May 10, 1865. Davis was locked up at Fortress Monroe on the coast of Virginia while Lubbock was imprisoned at Fort Delaware, a US Army prison at Pea Patch Island on the Delaware River. Lubbock was held in solitary confinement at Fort Delaware for more than seven months before being paroled.

Lubbock was born October 16, 1815, in Beaufort, South Carolina, the oldest son of Dr. Henry Thomas Willis Lubbock and Susan Ann Saltus Lubbock. When his father died in 1828, Lubbock quit school to work at a hardware store. During his time working in James H. Merritt's hardware business, he joined the Young Men's States' Rights Association. At seventeen, he was made secretary of the organization. Lubbock became a staunch states' rights advocate and a Democrat. He was a key figure in establishing the Democratic Party in Texas.

In 1832, Lubbock moved to Hamburg, South Carolina, where he was placed in charge of a large cotton warehouse attached to a general merchandising store. From Hamburg, Lubbock moved to New Orleans, where he and a friend opened a wholesale pharmaceuticals business. His brother Thomas Lubbock, whom

the city of Lubbock is named after, joined him in New Orleans after their mother's death in 1835. Like many others living in New Orleans at the time, Thomas became enamored with the Texas fight for independence against Mexico. With Francis Lubbock's help, Thomas joined the New Orleans Greys before they marched to the Siege of Bexar.

Lubbock followed his brother to Texas in 1836 after independence, and he settled in the Houston area. He opened a general store and sat on a committee that formally organized the city of Houston.

In 1837, Republic of Texas President Sam Houston appointed him comptroller; then in 1841, he was elected clerk of the Harris County district, a position he held for sixteen years. In 1846, during his term as clerk, Lubbock purchased a four-hundred-acre ranch six miles from Houston, on Sims Bayou, where he raised Asiatic poultry and camels. At the end of his tenure as Harris County district clerk, Lubbock was elected to the office of lieutenant governor. He lost his bid for reelection in 1859.

In 1860, Lubbock served as a Texas delegate to the national Democratic convention in Charleston. It was to be a turning point in the secessionist movement. At the Charleston convention, delegates from many southern states walked out in opposition to the Democratic platform and to its presidential nominee, Stephen A. Douglas. The remaining delegates, after failing to nominate a candidate, adjourned to meet again in Baltimore in June. After another southern walkout at the Baltimore convention, the southern Democratic

Party faction nominated John C. Breckinridge at their convention in Richmond, Virginia, a convention chaired by Lubbock. This fracturing of the Democratic Party is often considered the first overt sign that Southern loyalty to the Union was faltering.

Lubbock returned to Texas and ran for governor, prevailing in one of the state's tightest races—he won by a mere 124 votes. Already anticipating attack by the Union, Lubbock made several moves aimed at defending the state against Union forces. He proposed a state foundry for manufacturing cannon and other weapons, founded a coast guard for defense against the Union Navy, and began exporting cotton through Mexico to avoid Union blockades.

After his term as governor ended in 1863, Lubbock was appointed lieutenant colonel and served as assistant adjutant general under Major General John Bankhead Magruder. Lubbock's duties were to organize troop transports and supply trains for the Red River Campaign against General Nathaniel Banks. Lubbock was later transferred to the Eighth Texas Cavalry Regiment under General Thomas Green, but Green soon died and Major General John A. Wharton became his commander. Lubbock helped supply additional Confederate troops from Texas until August 1864, when he was appointed aide-de-camp to Jefferson Davis.

Lubbock worked in various businesses in Galveston and Houston after the war and served as tax collector in Galveston. From 1878 to 1891, he served as state treasurer. From 1891 until his death, he lived in Austin, where he died on June 22, 1905, and was interred at the State Cemetery.

Lubbock's first wife, Adele F. Baron Lubbock, died in Houston in 1882; Lubbock requested that her remains be buried next to him at the Cemetery. Lubbock's second wife, Sarah Elizabeth Black Porter Lubbock, died in 1902 and was also buried at the State Cemetery. Lubbock was married a third time in 1903, shortly before his death. His third wife, Lou Scott, was not buried at the Cemetery.

Photograph by Laurence Parent

AUGUSTUS CARL BUCHEL

1813–1864

Augustus Carl Buchel was buried in 1864 at the State Cemetery after a lifetime of military service to six different armies. A forgotten Texas patriot, Buchel suffered a mortal wound at the Battle of Pleasant Hill in Louisiana during the Civil War and was buried at the Cemetery at a ceremony overseen by Lieutenant Governor Fletcher Stockdale.

Buchel, a German immigrant to Texas, served in the US Army during the Mexican War, organized a special Texan detachment to combat bandits on the Mexican border in service to his adopted homeland, and served in the Confederate States of America Army.

Buchel's name does not stand next to those of Stephen F. Austin, William Barrett Travis, or Sam Houston in the history books, but, according to historian Stanley S. McGowen, his story is just as interesting. In his article, "Augustus Buchel: A Forgotten Texas Patriot," McGowen notes that many Texas patriots became "inseparable from Texas myth and history, while others disappeared into the mists of time. Augustus Buchel disappeared in those mists, but his deeds merit a more suitable place in Texas history than that accorded to him by historians."[4]

Buchel was born in Guntersblum, Hesse, along the Rhine River, in what is now Germany. He entered the military academy at Darmstadt at fourteen and at eighteen was commissioned a second lieutenant of volunteers in the First Infantry Regiment of Hesse-Darmstadt. His term of service in that regiment is generally accepted to have ended in 1835. That same year Buchel traveled to Paris to study at L'Ecole Militaire, the national military school of France, founded by King Louis XV and attended by Napoleon Bonaparte. Buchel graduated in 1836 and received an appointment as a lieutenant in the French Foreign Legion.

Buchel saw action during the First Carlist War, a war of succession to the Spanish crown. Several European nations, including France, sent troops to fight on behalf of the infant queen Isabella II and her mother and regent Maria Christina. Buchel served at the Battle of Huesca, where royalist forces defeated the Carlists. He was awarded the Cross of San Fernando and given a knighthood for his actions in battle.

Buchel then pursued his military career in other parts of Europe and beyond. After his unit was disbanded in 1838, he traveled to Vienna. There he met a representative of the Ottoman Empire and was hired to train the empire's cavalry. Buchel rose to the rank of colonel and was granted the title of *Pasha*, probably as a gesture of respect, before leaving Ottoman service. By 1845, he had returned to Hesse.

Many accounts of Buchel's life suggest he killed an adversary in a duel after returning to Hesse. According to McGowen, Buchel had a reputation for dueling and had been involved in "several affairs of honor." A duel at Hesse may have played a part in Buchel's immigration to Texas. He and his brother Charles set out for the New World in 1845.

By October 1845, Buchel and his brother had settled near Karlshafen, the German settlement near Matagorda Bay (renamed Indianola in 1846). Buchel's brother began farming in DeWitt County, but

Augustus Carl Buchel, Civil War veteran and European soldier, died during the Red River Campaign of the Civil War while leading a charge at the Battle of Pleasant Hill in 1864. Used with the permission of Texas State Library and Archives Commission, Archives and Information Services Division, 1/102-64.

he returned to the military life at the eruption of the Mexican-American War. He organized a group of German settlers into what was later called Company H, First Brigade of Texas Volunteer Riflemen, under the command of Colonel Albert Sidney Johnston. The volunteers disbanded after their ninety-day enlistment expired, but Buchel remained on, and, probably because of his past service and fluency in Spanish, was appointed to General Zachary Taylor's staff.

He was present at the Battle of Buena Vista, where he was said to have played an important role in military strategy. General Taylor was grateful for Buchel's help and planned to reward him after being elected president of the United States, according to Buchel's eulogy, delivered by Texas Lieutenant Governor Fletcher Stockdale. Stockdale wrote, "I have been informed that such was Taylor's appreciation of his capacity and qualifications, that he intended after he was chosen President of the United States, to make him Minister to Brazil, which was only prevented by the untimely death of that President."

Buchel's role in US history was recognized, however, by Taylor's successor, Franklin Pierce. The new president appointed Buchel to a somewhat lesser position—customs inspector at the port of Lavaca. While living there, Buchel also became involved in the lumber and building material business, but was called again to protect his territory from invaders in 1859. At the time, a group of Mexican bandits, led by Juan N. Cortina, conducted raids along the Rio Grande and around Brownsville that became collectively known as the "Cortina Wars." Buchel organized the Indianola Volunteers to guard the area from these predators. The Volunteers, however, never engaged in actual combat, and in 1860 they disbanded.

When the Civil War broke out, Buchel resumed military service by joining the Texas militia. Late in 1861, he was appointed lieutenant colonel of the Third Texas Infantry and served as the commander of Fort Brown in South Texas. Buchel was responsible for preventing invasions of the Rio Grande Valley and preserving the overland cotton trade to Mexico. He was transferred to the Gulf Coast by 1863 and saw combat several times against invading Union forces. When Union forces threatened to invade Louisiana, Buchel was transferred there. He fought extensively in the Red River Campaign.

Buchel died while leading three hundred men in a dismounted charge at Pleasant Hill on April 9, 1864. According to McGowen, Buchel remained on his horse to lead his men and thus made himself an easy target—the career military man was shot seven times. His troops took him to Mansfield, where he died of his wounds. Although Buchel had been appointed a brigadier general earlier in the campaign, his appointment was never confirmed and he died with the rank of colonel. The same year, Buchel's remains were transported to the Texas State Cemetery where he was buried with honors.

A white stone marker was erected on Buchel's grave and inscribed with this sentiment: "We know that those who for their country die, through glory live again immortally."

EDMUND J. DAVIS

1827–1883

REPUBLIC HILL, SECTION 1 (C1), ROW Q, PLOT 19

Edmund J. Davis, widely reviled in his lifetime, was a Reconstruction governor of Texas. He died in Austin in 1883, mostly unmourned, and was buried at the State Cemetery for his service as governor. Initially, his grave was topped by a modest marker, although not modest enough for many Texans who felt he was a traitor because he raised a cavalry regiment that fought for the Union during the Civil War. His brother, however, erected a massive gray granite monument on his grave shortly after Davis's death to replace the original simple headstone. At more than thirty feet, it remains the tallest marker in the Cemetery.

Davis is a controversial figure in Texas history, and not just because of his role in Reconstruction. He was elected governor in 1869 by eight hundred votes over Andrew Jackson Hamilton, a fellow Republican. Many historians cite voter fraud, intimidation, and other irregularities on both sides. At the time of the election, matters were already in upheaval: Governor E. M. Pease had resigned prior to the election when US Army General J. J. Reynolds ordered a new list of registered voters drawn up. That effectively eliminated voters who might have cast their ballot for Hamilton. US troops were also stationed at many polling places. Some voters claimed the troops prevented Democrats from voting.

Davis was declared the winner of the election, but that didn't improve his popularity—and neither did some of the bills he introduced in the legislature that were intended to consolidate gubernatorial powers. Bills passed during Davis's term included a militia bill requiring men between ages eighteen and forty-five to serve in a state militia under the command of the governor's office and another that allowed the governor to declare martial law in any county.

A state police force was established during Davis's administration. He offended opponents (and made a few more) by allowing blacks and Hispanics into the force, which was anathema to ex-Confederate sympathizers still smarting from the outcome of the Civil War. The reputation of the state police wasn't a sterling one at the time—charges of corruption were rampant, particularly after one prominent member of the force embezzled a large amount of money and fled the state.

There is some evidence that the state police force had a positive impact on society at the time. In a *Handbook of Texas* article, John G. Johnson notes that the police were effective in arresting violent criminals. "In the first month," he writes, "the force made 978 arrests, 109 for murder and 130 for attempted murder. By 1872, arrests totaled 6,820—587 for murder, 760 for attempted murder, and 1,748 for other felonies. The value of recovered stolen property was $200,000. The largest number of arrests in any one year was 3,602 in 1871."[5]

The Enabling Act and the Printing Act also proved controversial. The Enabling Act allowed the governor to appoint people to various state and local government positions that previously had been held by elected officials. Because the first state elections after readmission to the Union had been postponed for a year (to November 1872), this act gave the governor an extraordinary

The grave of Edmund J. Davis, the largest at the Texas State Cemetery, was erected by his brother after Davis's death in 1883. Photograph by Will Erwin.

opportunity to appoint officeholders. Detractors argued that Davis used the law liberally and appointed his friends to powerful positions in government. The Printing Act doled out state money to regional newspapers to print official notices. Critics charged that this law used patronage to create a state-controlled press.

Davis found support for some of the changes he instituted, such as the establishment of the homestead exemption and policies encouraging the construction of railroads and other infrastructure. However, his impact—positive or not—in Texas was quickly negated. Many laws passed during his term, including the state police law and a centralized public school system, were repealed in the succeeding administration.

Davis ran for reelection in 1873 against Democrat and ex-Confederate Richard Coke and was defeated by a two-to-one margin in an election as tainted by claims of intimidation and fraud as the 1869 gubernatorial race. Davis challenged the results. He believed the election was illegal and should have been held the following year. The challenge was dubbed the Coke-Davis controversy—and for a short time, Texas had two governors.

Coke took office in January 15, 1874, at the Capitol, but Davis refused to leave. The Texas Supreme Court ruled in Davis's favor, and he held that the election itself was illegal. Davis's ouster was complete only after he sent a telegram to Republican President Ulysses S. Grant asking for aid. Grant, not inclined to interfere in local problems, replied that the election was the will of the people and suggested that Davis concede. Davis complied and left office on January 19.

Coke and a Democratic legislature undid or modified many of Davis's policies. The Democrats decentralized power and passed a new Constitution in 1875 that weakened the power of the governor and state government in general. Davis was the last Republican governor of Texas until William Clements was elected in 1978.

Davis sought election to various posts throughout the rest of his life, but none of his campaigns for public office were successful. He served as head of the Republican Party in Texas from 1875 until his death in Austin in 1883.

Davis's marker will continue to be the tallest at the State Cemetery. After the monument was erected, a Cemetery rule was enacted decreeing no monument could be as tall as his.

CHAPTER FOUR

PUBLIC

★

OFFICIALS

INTRODUCTION BY SECRETARY DON EVANS

JUDGE
W. L. DAVIDSON
NOVEMBER 5, 1845
JANUARY 25, 1921

"ERECTED BY THE LAWYERS OF TEXAS
IN MEMORY OF A JUST JUDGE."

DESIGNED & EXECUTED
BY A. STASSWENDER
AUSTIN TEXAS

WILLIAM LEWIS DAVIDSON
NOVEMBER 5, 1845
JANUARY 25, 1921

Grave of William Lewis Davidson, judge and Confederate veteran. Davidson suffered a stroke while fishing in Austin and drowned on January 25, 1921. He was interred in the State Cemetery. Photograph by Laurence Parent.

INTRODUCTION

BY SECRETARY DON EVANS

Don Evans was the secretary of the United States Department of Commerce during President George W. Bush's first term. He also served on the University of Texas Board of Regents. He is a native Texan and graduated from the University of Texas.

Many states are defined by land or resources or industry. Texas is defined by leaders.

From the men who died at the Alamo to the wildcatters who created the oil industry to the scientists at NASA who explore the skies and the heavens, Texans have always been willing to take the reins and ride herd. We've never been willing to stand back and follow; we've always had folks who wanted to stand up and lead.

And nowhere is that more evident than in our public officials. We have a great state in large part because we've had great public officials who have led us well. These weren't politicians doing what was safe or shrewd; these were leaders doing what was right.

These public officials deserve our attention. More than that, they deserve our reflection. From their example we can draw inspiration for our own time and our own challenges. "Ma" and "Pa" Ferguson were dedicated populists who believed in bettering the lives of ordinary Texans. James Pinckney Henderson was a skilled negotiator who secured diplomatic recognition from England and France while serving as secretary of state for the Republic of Texas. Barbara Jordan was a principled defender of the civil rights of all Americans. And Bob

Bullock was a shrewd lieutenant governor who worked across the aisle with Governor George W. Bush to create an era of progress and prosperity for Texas in the 1990s.

Each of these individuals blazed his or her own trail. But all shared the same gift of leadership. All knew how to turn an obstacle into an opportunity. All wanted to make decisions today that would create an even better tomorrow. And that's what leadership is about. It's doing what's right instead of what's popular; it's about rejecting what is and working for what should be. Texas has been blessed to have many such leaders. And several of them can be now found resting at the Texas State Cemetery. Though they are gone, they are not forgotten. We are a better state and a better people because of the leadership of these great Texans.

★

A portrait of Republic Hill, including the monument to Stephen F. Austin and the grave of Barbara Jordan, at sunset. Photograph by Laurence Parent.

A replica Charles Umlauf sculpture of the Virgin Mary at the grave of former governor Allan Shivers and his wife Marialice. Photograph by Will Erwin.

The Texas State Cemetery was created to honor the sacrifices made by the men who established and later shaped Texas laws and culture. The Republic of Texas public officials set a high standard for Texas. Those who followed have had to work hard, be dedicated, and be innovative to maintain that high standard. The following public officials have done just that for our great state.

EDWARD BURLESON

1798–1851

REPUBLIC HILL, SECTION 1 (C1), ROW Q, PLOT 13

It is because of the overwhelming respect in which Edward Burleson, vice president of the Republic of Texas and veteran of the Battle of San Jacinto, was held that the State Cemetery exists today. Burleson died unexpectedly in Austin after a bout with pneumonia in the winter of 1851. On the day of his death, the Texas Legislature went into a special session to eulogize him. In proceedings that lasted much of the day, it was decided that a special state burying ground should be founded for Burleson's interment.

A patch of land located east of the Capitol was donated to the state by Representative Andrew Jackson Hamilton for Burleson's burying place. Two days later, Burleson was interred at the top of the highest hill on the property and became the first person buried at the Texas State Cemetery.

Burleson was born in 1798 in North Carolina to US Army Captain James Burleson and Elizabeth Shipman Burleson. At the age of fourteen, he fought in the War of 1812 alongside his father. James and Edward Burleson both served under General Andrew Jackson at the Battle of New Orleans in January 1815, the last major battle of the war.

Burleson pursued his military career wherever his family settled. On October 20, 1817, he was appointed a captain of militia in Howard County, Missouri; he was commissioned colonel on June 13, 1821, in Saline County, Missouri; and he was colonel of militia from 1823 to 1830 in Hardeman County, Tennessee. He married Sarah Griffith Owen on April 25, 1816, shortly after the Burleson clan moved to Missouri.

Burleson arrived in Texas in May 1830, one of the first Burlesons to move to Texas. His father followed a year later. Other Burleson relatives fought in the Texas independence movement: Edward's sons Aaron B. and Jonathan served in the Texas War for Independence, and a grandson, Edward Burleson Jr., fought in the Texas War for Independence and the Civil War.

However, it was Edward Burleson who put an indelible stamp on Texas history. He was appointed to a governing council, the *ayuntamiento,* in August 1832. The council governed the counties of Austin, Bexar, Goliad, and Guadalupe. On December 7, 1832, he was elected lieutenant colonel of the militia of one of Stephen F. Austin's original colonies.

His colonial Texas military experience involved de-

fending settlers from Indian raids from 1832 to 1840. He participated in several battles between the Republic of Texas and the Comanche, Cherokee, and other tribes.

When tensions between the Texans and the Mexican government came to a head in 1835, Burleson was appointed a lieutenant colonel in Stephen F. Austin's fledgling army. He was also appointed to be a delegate to the Consultation of 1835, the Texans' first attempts at a provisional government, but he was unable to attend.

During the independence movement, Burleson's role was to be much greater as a military leader for the Texas army rather than as a political leader. On November 24, 1835, he became general of the volunteer army when Stephen F. Austin traveled to the United States to request aid. Burleson took command of the Texas army at the Siege of Bexar.

Before the end of the year, he was appointed commander in chief of the army by the Texas provisional government. By December 14, he had captured Bexar, and the volunteer army disbanded a week later. Burleson raised a volunteer company and rode to Gonzales in February 1836, while the siege of the Alamo was under way. By March 10, in Gonzales, he was elected colonel of the infantry, First Regiment, Texas Volunteers. It is likely that during this time the bitter rivalry between Burleson and Sam Houston began.

The reasons are somewhat unclear, but tension surfaced at first with Houston's nagging criticism of Burleson's credibility as a leader. Burleson was in charge of the largest contingent of volunteer soldiers in the march toward San Jacinto and the culminating battle of the Texas independence movement. Houston questioned the discipline of Burleson's soldiers and their ability to fight a pitched battle against Santa Anna's trained soldiers. In turn, Burleson's men grumbled about the continuing retreat of the Houston-led army in the face of the Mexican advance. Although some critics called Houston's bravery into question, Burleson—who may have concurred—never did so openly.

Despite the lack of good feeling between the two, the Battle of San Jacinto was a rout. In fewer than twenty minutes, the Texans took the Mexican position, killing more than six hundred and capturing more than

Photograph by Will Erwin

seven hundred. Burleson's regiment led the charge, and he personally accepted the surrender of General Juan N. Almonte.

Burleson's military service continued after Texas became a republic, and so did Houston's dislike for him. In fact, it was Burleson's actions against the Cherokee that finally turned the rivalry between Houston and him into hatred. Burleson led Texas troops against the Cherokee and defeated them at Pecan Bayou in 1839. This outraged Houston, a Cherokee citizen and a staunch proponent of peace between them and Anglo settlers. Burleson sealed Houston's hatred of him forever, though, by sending him the defeated chief's scalp.

During two Mexican invasions of the state—one under Rafael Vásquez and the other under Adrián Woll—Burleson raised troops for the state's defense. Both times, he was superseded by then-President Houston. After being relieved of command by Alexander Somervell during the 1842 Woll invasion, Burleson made his famous speech regarding the Alamo: "though Thermopylae had her messenger of defeat, the Alamo had none," referring to the Battle of Thermopylae in 48 BC, one of the most famous last stands in history in which a Greek garrison of a few thousand soldiers was vastly outnumbered by Persian invading troops.

Burleson's final military service came after the an-nexation of Texas to the United States. The United States declared war after a Mexican incursion across the Rio Grande. A major in the US Army and a senior aide-de-camp to General Zachary Taylor, Burleson served at the Battle of Buena Vista and acted as an army spy.

Though Burleson's military contributions to the State of Texas and the Republic are many, he was also a politician and policy maker. He served in Texas's first three Republican congresses, was elected vice president of the Republic in 1842, and was a state senator in the first Texas Senate; in addition, he surveyed and helped lay out the city plan for Waterloo (now Austin). Burleson founded Hays County and donated the land for the courthouse. When he died, he was president pro tem of the Senate.

Burleson was never considered an educated or learned man, but those who knew and respected him touted his common sense and bravery. The graveside eulogy by the Reverend E. Fontaine reflected the attitude of many Texans toward Burleson: "Without the advantage of a liberal education, self-taught and self-made," said Fontaine, "he received from nature's God endowments which collegiate learning could not give him, however it might have refined and improved the gifts—goodness of heart and greatness of soul; courage and fortitude."[1]

JAMES EDWARD FERGUSON

1871–1944

AND

MIRIAM AMANDA WALLACE FERGUSON

1875–1961

REPUBLIC HILL, SECTION 2 (C2), ROW H, PLOTS 1 AND 2

James Edward Ferguson and Miriam Anderson Wallace Ferguson were connected in life by marriage and connected in Texas history by more than their nicknames, "Ma" and "Pa." Populists at heart, the Fergusons brought a mixed, if colorful, legacy to the state's history. Both have the distinction of being "firsts": Miriam was the first woman elected governor of Texas and James was the first—and only—Texas governor to be impeached.

James Ferguson, a banker from Temple, defeated Thomas H. Ball to become governor of Texas in 1914. During his first term, Ferguson championed education. He helped pass legislation to send aid to rural schools, establish the Austin State School, fund college building programs, and approve large appropriations for education.

Ferguson's opponent in the 1917 election was Charles H. Morris, an obscure Prohibitionist, deemed a sure loser by many political pundits in the state. They were right, and as predicted, Ferguson was reelected. But the honeymoon was brief.

A confrontation between the governor and the University of Texas brought to light allegations of corruption that had surfaced in the last election. Ferguson asked for the dismissal of several liberal professors on the staff at UT, but President Robert E. Vinson refused to comply. In retaliation, Ferguson vetoed the university's appropriation bill for the following biennium. His actions sparked protests by students and outraged university alumni, and caused unhappiness in the legislative ranks. The UT decision and ever-deepening troubles at Ferguson's bank in Temple brought the governor's woes to a head on July 21, 1917, when he was summoned to appear before a Travis County grand jury. He was indicted on nine charges, including misapplication of funds and embezzlement.

The Speaker of the House called the legislature into special session shortly thereafter—an act that was unconstitutional because only the governor can call a special session—to consider the matter of impeachment. The legality of the special session was not called into question because Ferguson himself backed the call, believing the legislature would not go through with impeachment.

The House spent a considerable amount of time reviewing the charges against the governor and in the end prepared twenty-one articles of impeachment. The Senate convicted Ferguson on ten of the charges, including misapplication of state funds. Perhaps most damning, though, was the charge of accepting $156,000

James Edward Ferguson, twenty-sixth governor of Texas and known as "Pa" Ferguson in Texas history. Courtesy of the Daughters of the Republic of Texas.

Miriam Amanda Wallace Ferguson, first woman governor of Texas, died in 1961 and was buried next to her husband and twenty-sixth governor of Texas, James Edward Ferguson. Used with the permission of Texas State Library and Archives Commission, Archives and Information Services Division, 1981/57-18.

from an undisclosed source, most likely an interest related to the alcoholic beverage industry.

Ferguson resigned September 24, 1917, before the verdict could be read. He reasoned that if he was not governor the charges might not apply, and he could thus avoid the most serious punishment of being banned from holding public office. His resignation didn't move the Senate. The punishment handed down by the Senate was Ferguson's removal from office and a permanent ban barring him from holding any public office. Lieutenant Governor William Hobby was appointed to fill the gubernatorial vacancy.

Ferguson held that the ban was illegal and sought the Democratic nomination for governor in 1918, only to be beaten by Hobby in the primary. The defeat didn't deter Ferguson; he ran for president in 1920 on the American Party ticket but received less than 2 percent of the vote. He ran again for office in 1922, this time for the US Senate against Earle B. Mayfield, a race he also lost.

Not one to take "no" for an answer, Ferguson attempted to have his name put on the Democratic ticket for governor in 1924. The move was unsuccessful, but the resourceful Ferguson told a newspaper reporter that his wife was going to run for governor, something he neglected to tell her.

At first, Miriam Ferguson was angry with her husband, according to her biographers May Nelson Paulissen and Carl McQueary. However, she began to enjoy the idea and actively campaigned alongside her husband. It was during this campaign that "Ma" Ferguson received her nickname. The former governor used the term in a speech and it stuck.

James Ferguson was the active force behind the campaign, saying in a speech, "You'll get two governors for the price of one. I'll tell her what to sign and what not to sign." Miriam Ferguson had other ideas and later promised, "If I am elected, I am going to be governor. To Jim belongs [sic] only the honors that go with being the husband of the governor. He will be my right hand man, that's all, just like I was his when he was governor."[2]

Regardless of the rhetoric, James Ferguson was the pilot of Miriam's political career. She defeated the Ku Klux Klan–endorsed candidate Felix Robertson and became one of the first female governors in the country. As governor, Miriam Ferguson oversaw anti-Klan legislation, cut overall spending, and reformed the prison system.

However, the controversy that ended James Ferguson's official political career continued to dog his wife's as well, and Miriam was not reelected. She left office amid scandals of political patronage, abuses in the highway department, and accusations of granting excessive pardons.

Miriam Ferguson sought the governor's office again in 1930, but was unsuccessful. She successfully ran for the office in 1932 and tried again in 1940 but was not elected.

James Ferguson died in 1944 and was interred at the Texas State Cemetery. Miriam Ferguson retired from public life after her husband's death and lived in Austin, where she died in 1961. She was buried next to her husband at the Cemetery.

LIFE'S · RACE · WELL · RUN
LIFE'S · WORK · WELL · DONE
LIFE'S · VICTORY · WON
NOW · COMETH · REST

JAMES PINCKNEY HENDERSON
1808–1858

REPUBLIC HILL, SECTION 2 (C2), ROW M, PLOT 5

On February 19, 1846, James Pinckney Henderson was inaugurated the first governor of the state of Texas in a ceremony that retired the flag of the Republic of Texas and raised the United States flag as Texas became the twenty-ninth state in the Union.

Henderson was born March 31, 1808, in Lincolnton, North Carolina. He studied law at the University of North Carolina and was licensed to practice in 1829. While pursuing his profession in North Carolina, Henderson made acquaintance with Ashbel Smith, another young lawyer who would later contribute to the development of the state of Texas.

Henderson subsequently moved to Mississippi, where he practiced law, and then to Texas. Immediately commissioned a general in the Republic of Texas Army, he was sent back to the United States to raise funds and troops for Texas's fight for independence. Henderson already had a reputation for getting results, and his record of achievement was growing daily. When President Sam Houston set up his first administration, Henderson was appointed attorney general of the new Republic of Texas. Houston called Henderson "an individual possessing moral worth, genius and talents proper to the discharge of the duties of that office."[3]

The course of Henderson's career changed three times due to a colleague's death. Sam Houston named Texas "patriarch" and hero Stephen F. Austin to be the secretary of state of the new Republic, but Austin served only a few months, dying of pneumonia on December 27, 1836. Henderson took Austin's place in that

office. He faced several problems associated with the new government's struggle for international credibility. The most pressing issues included securing loans from the United States and European countries and acquiring recognition as a sovereign state.

In 1837, Henderson was appointed Texas's minister to England and France, and he traveled to the two countries to secure treaties of recognition for Texas. England, skeptical that Texas could defend itself against Mexico, was hesitant to recognize the new republic. The fact that Texas supported slavery was not a point in its favor, either. However, Henderson was persistent and achieved a working compromise: England still considered Texas a part of Mexico but agreed to trade with the Republic as an independent nation.

Henderson then proceeded to France in 1838 to persuade that government to recognize Texas independence. While there, Henderson found that Mexico would again play a major role in his negotiations: France and Mexico were in a bitter dispute over the payment of damages to French landowners who had been denied payment for the sale of their property in Mexico. One of Henderson's main selling points was the recognition of the Republic by the United States, which eased France's uncertainty that annexation might not occur.

Finally, after much negotiation, a treaty was signed by King Louis Phillipe, the French Foreign Minister Marshall Soult, and Henderson. France was the first European country to recognize Texas independence.

Henderson returned to Texas to practice law in 1840 and also to marry his fiancée, Frances Cox. Meanwhile,

the Republic was busy preparing for annexation to the United States, and Henderson was a delegate to the Convention of 1845, where a new state constitution was to be written. He also used the opportunity to consider running for Congress. As fate would have it, Henderson's law partner, Kenneth L. Anderson, who was a candidate for governor, died suddenly. For the second time, death derailed Henderson's career plans. He took his partner's place as a candidate and, in 1845, was elected governor of Texas by an overwhelming majority.

As governor, Henderson faced many challenges, not the least of which was the ever-present issue of Mexico. By the end of April 1846, the United States was at war with Mexico. US General Zachary Taylor called for a group of Texas volunteers to be formed. The Texas Legislature placed Henderson in command, and he was commissioned major general of the Texas volunteer forces. Proving he could succeed on the battlefield as well as in the political arena, he played a vital role in capturing Monterrey during the Mexican-American War. After the war ended, Henderson returned to Austin and his more peaceful duties as governor. He did not run for reelection and returned to San Augustine to once again practice law.

Tragedy again entangled Henderson when, in 1857, his longtime friend and law partner US Senator Thomas J. Rusk committed suicide. For the third time, Henderson's career plans changed when the Texas Legislature elected him to fill the seat left vacant by Rusk's death. Henderson, however, would not serve long: he fell ill and died on June 4, 1858, fewer than seven months after he had taken office. He was buried at the Congressional Cemetery in Washington, DC. In 1930, the State of Texas had his remains disinterred and moved to the Texas State Cemetery. His wife later remarried and is buried in New Jersey with her second husband.

BARBARA JORDAN

1936–1996

REPUBLIC HILL, SECTION 1 (C1), ROW N, PLOT 6

Barbara Jordan, the first black woman elected to the Texas Senate and the first black woman from the South to serve in the US House of Representatives, died in 1996 after a life of service to the public. Jordan was internationally revered for her gift of speaking and the distinctive sound of her voice.

Jordan was born in Houston's Fifth Ward and attended Texas public schools. She graduated from Texas Southern University and then earned a law degree from Boston University in 1959. But Jordan was more than a good student—she was a compelling and provocative public speaker, even early in life. While still in school, Jordan earned many first-place trophies for debate and oratory. She was also a teacher—at the beginning of her career and at the end. Between her graduation from law school and her return to her hometown of Houston, she taught at the Tuskegee Institute in Alabama.

Jordan attempted to enter politics during the 1960s, but lost two elections before she was finally elected to the Texas Senate in 1967. Lyndon Johnson was a strong advocate for Jordan, and he used his influence to help her campaigns. When the Texas Legislature convened in special session in March 1972, Senator Jordan was unanimously elected president pro tempore—the first person of her race and gender to hold the post.

She was elected to the US House of Representatives in 1972 and quickly rose to a position of prominence. She was named to the venerable House Judiciary Committee in 1974, an honor for a young congresswoman. From that committee, Jordan gained the national spotlight after speaking in the 1974 Watergate hearings. She began with these remarks:

> Earlier today we heard the beginning of the Preamble to the Constitution of the United States, "We, the people." It is a very eloquent beginning. But when that document was completed, on the seventeenth of September in 1787, I was not included in that We, the people. I felt somehow for many years that George Washington and Alexander Hamilton just left me out by mistake. But through the process of amendment, interpretation, and court decision I have finally been included in We, the people. Today I am an inquisitor. I believe hyperbole would not be fictional and would not overstate the solemnness that I feel right now. My faith in the Constitution is whole, it is complete, it is total. I am not going to sit here and be an idle spectator to the diminution, the subversion, the destruction of the Constitution.[4]

In 1976, Jordan became the first woman to speak at the Democratic National Convention—a speech widely remembered as the highlight of the convention that nominated Jimmy Carter for the presidency. Among many themes Jordan addressed was the soundness of the United States government. "We cannot," she said, "improve on the system of government handed down to us by the founders of the Republic, there is no way to improve upon that. But what we can do is to find new ways to implement that system and realize our destiny."[5] Later in that same speech, Jordan went on to say:

Barbara Charline Jordan, the first black woman from the South to be elected to Congress, died in 1996. Image provided by the State Preservation Board, Austin, Texas.

A nation is formed by the willingness of each of us to share in the responsibility for upholding the common good. A government is invigorated when each one of us is willing to participate in shaping the future of this nation. In this election year, we must define the "common good" and begin again to shape a common future. Let each person do his or her part. If one citizen is unwilling to participate, all of us are going to suffer. For the American idea, though it is shared by all of us, is realized in each one of us.[6]

Following her retirement from the United States Congress, Jordan accepted a teaching position at the LBJ School of Public Affairs at the University of Texas at Austin.

Though in failing health, Jordan once again spoke at the Democratic convention. Among the highlights of her 1992 speech was a call for unity. "We must," she reminded us, "change that deleterious environment of the '80s, that environment which was characterized by greed, and hatred, and selfishness, and mega-mergers, and debt overhang. Change it to what? Change that environment of the '80s to an environment which is characterized by a devotion to the public interest, public service, tolerance, and love. Love. Love. Love."[7]

Shortly after Jordan's death in 1996, Senator Barbara Boxer of California delivered an address to the US Senate, eulogizing the Texan:

Barbara Jordan was a voice for common ground, for the ties that bind. Hers were powerful, healing, uplifting words that challenged and inspired women and minorities, indeed all Americans, to reach for something higher and to believe in themselves and their own ability to change the world and make it a better place. Her life was a testament to that idea. A nation mourns a great loss, but it is my hope that the spirit of Barbara Jordan will live on forever in the many Americans who have been touched deeply by her powerful words and exemplary life. I certainly have been.[8]

Boxer was one of many to mourn and eulogize Jordan after her death. Congresswoman Sheila Jackson Lee of Texas said:

Barbara Jordan was a lawyer, legislator, scholar, author, and presidential adviser. She was immensely gifted, and used every bit of her talent and skill to address, improve, and dignify the conditions of human life. In the tradition of Frederick Douglass, Martin Luther King, and Thurgood Marshall, she challenged the Federal Government and the American people to uphold the principles set forth in the American Constitution.[9]

Jordan was inducted into the National Women's Hall of Fame in 1990 and awarded the Presidential Medal of Freedom in 1994. She suffered from a number of ailments in her later years, including a form of multiple sclerosis, and was confined to a wheelchair, but even so she insisted on enjoying her life. During her Austin years, she was a beloved fixture on the sidelines of the women's basketball games at the University of Texas.

In death, as in her life, Barbara Jordan was a trailblazer: she was the first black woman to be buried at the Texas State Cemetery. She rests near Stephen F. Austin in a place of honor on the highest hill. Her headstone reads "Eloquent Champion of Ethics and Justice."

Jordan will be remembered for the power and passion of her speeches, and, most of all, for her ability to present even the most complex ideas clearly and vividly. Her faith in America was vast, and her belief in the American people was boundless. "What the people want is very simple," said Jordan. "They want an America as good as its promise."

ROBERT ALLAN SHIVERS

1907–1985

REPUBLIC HILL, SECTION 1 (C1), ROW Q, PLOT 1

Robert Allan Shivers was governor from 1949 to 1957. He assumed the position when Governor Beauford H. Jester died in office. Shivers was reelected three times and served for seven and a half years—the longest-serving governor in the history of the state at the time. An advisor to state and national politicians of both parties, Shivers is widely credited with laying the seeds for the resurgence of the Republican Party in Texas.

Shivers was born in Lufkin and raised in Woodville. He moved with his family to Port Arthur, where he graduated from high school. Shivers entered college at the University of Texas, but dropped out after his first year to work at an oil refinery in Port Arthur. In 1928, he reentered the university and graduated with a bachelor's degree in the same year; he also passed the state bar exam, although he did not receive his law degree until two years later.

In 1934, Shivers was elected to the Texas Senate at the age of twenty-seven and achieved the unique status of being the youngest person ever elected to the Senate. Three years later, he married Marialice Shary. After World War II broke out, Shivers entered the service in 1943 and served in North Africa, Italy, France, and Germany. Honorably discharged in 1945 with the rank of major, he came home bearing the Bronze Star and five battle stars. Although Shivers left Texas politics behind him to serve in the war, he returned with an eye toward the lieutenant governor's office, and, in 1946, he was elected to the post.

Friendships forged during the war years had a last-ing effect on the young politician. Shivers became acquainted with General Dwight D. Eisenhower and they became lifelong friends. It was a relationship that affected Shivers and his politics—and eventually Texas politics—profoundly.

A canny politician, Shivers was instrumental in President Eisenhower's electoral victory in Texas in 1952, despite Eisenhower being a Republican and Texas being a historically Democratic state. Shivers led the charge for Eisenhower in his home state and many Democrats followed. Those who crossed party lines even had their own moniker, "Shivercrats," and were neither Democrat nor Republican. Although officially still a Democrat, Shivers was listed on the ballot as a nominee of both parties in the gubernatorial election that year. The achievement was notable and both *Time* and *Newsweek* magazines featured Shivers on their covers.

As a member and chairman of the Interstate Oil Compact Commission, Shivers, along with politicians in many other states, had long opposed federal claims to title over coastal tidelands and the oilfields they contained. Reclaiming tidelands areas for state jurisdiction would have a lucrative outcome for states like Texas with offshore oil deposits. In return for Shivers's support in the 1952 presidential election, Eisenhower promised to deed the tidelands to the states affected.

Eisenhower, as good as his word, signed the tidelands legislation into law in 1953. Texas used the new revenue from leases, rentals, and royalties on the tidelands property to help fund schools in Texas. Since the rights were granted, Texas has reaped billions of dollars in revenue.

Shivers's other accomplishments as governor included the improvement of retirement benefits for state employees and a reorganized state educational program. In addition, he oversaw the reform of the jury system in Texas to allow women to serve on grand juries and on criminal and civil juries. In 1951, Shivers was able to push legislative redistricting, the first redistricting in thirty years for Texas.

Shivers retired from government service in 1957, but he remained active behind the scenes. He worked to help Richard Nixon become president and, ever the diplomatic politician, he was offered cabinet positions by two diversely different presidents, Nixon and Lyndon Johnson.

In 1973, Shivers was appointed to a six-year term to the University of Texas Board of Regents, where he served as chairman for four years. During this time, he donated his Austin home, the former residence of Reconstruction Governor E. M. Pease, to the university. In 1980, he was instrumental in securing a five-million-dollar grant for the University of Texas College of Communication, which soon thereafter established an endowed chair of journalism in his honor.

Shivers died unexpectedly in 1985 and was interred at the State Cemetery. His wife died in 1996 and was buried next to Shivers beneath a pink granite marker topped by a replica of Texas sculptor Charles Umlauf's *Spirit of Flight* and anchored at the base by a replica of Umlauf's *Maria Regina*.

JOHN BOWDEN CONNALLY JR.

1917–1993

REPUBLIC HILL, SECTION 2 (C2), ROW P, PLOT 9

John Connally, Texas governor, secretary of the navy, secretary of the treasury, and one-time presidential hopeful, is considered by many to be one of Texas's greatest governors. In 1999, *Texas Monthly* magazine selected him as the foremost Texas governor of the twentieth century. He is certainly one of the most memorable on a national level. Most Americans remember him as a passenger in John F. Kennedy's limousine when Kennedy was assassinated in Dallas.

Connally joined with influential Texan Lyndon B. Johnson early in their political careers. When Johnson became president, many political insiders considered Connally a rising star and a good bet for a future election to the highest office in the land.

Connally's political career began in 1939 when he worked as an assistant in then-Congressman Johnson's office. Connally married Idanell Brill shortly after beginning work for Johnson. He joined the Navy in 1940 and served in nine major sea battles in both the Pacific and European theaters and was awarded a Bronze Star and the Legion of Merit.

After returning home from the war, Connally and a group of veterans purchased and operated Austin radio station KVET. During this period, Connally served as campaign manager in Johnson's 1946 reelection bid for Congress, as well as his 1948 Senate race—a race remembered more for the scandals associated with it than for anything else. When Johnson was elected, Connally became an aide in his mentor's office.

From 1952 until 1960, Connally went to work for Sid W. Richardson and Perry R. Bass as their attorney and was active in the management of broadcasting, real estate, retail sales, oil and gas, ranching, manufacturing, and investment interests. Richardson, an influential oilman, died in 1960, and Connally served as the executor of his estate.

When John F. Kennedy was elected president in 1960, he tapped Connally for the post of secretary of the navy. Connally accepted, but resigned to run for governor of Texas in 1962. Connally, a Democrat, was elected from a field of five other candidates, many—including Texas attorney general Will Wilson—with better name recognition than the former navy secretary.

Shortly after his election as governor, Connally acquired an indelible position in the national consciousness. The Democratic Party had barely won the state in the 1962 midterm election, and fund-raising efforts for the upcoming campaign were sluggish. President Kennedy, anxious to improve his standing in the state, made the fateful decision to visit Texas before the 1964 presidential election. Many historians suggest that Kennedy also visited Dallas to mend fences among Texas's three most powerful—and incompatible—politicians: Senator Ralph Yarborough on one side, and Governor Connally and Vice President Johnson on the other. Connally denied this theory on numerous occasions.

Kennedy planned to visit several parts of the state on November 22, 1963. On the tour through Dallas, Connally rode in a convertible limousine with the president. The events have been replayed countless times in the press, in schools, and for conspiracy buff panels. From the Texas School Book Depository facing

John Bowden Connally Jr.,
governor of Texas and one-time US
presidential hopeful, died in 1993
and was interred at a place of honor
at the Texas State Cemetery. Image
provided by the State Preservation
Board, Austin, Texas.

Dealey Plaza in downtown Dallas, Lee Harvey Oswald opened fire on the presidential entourage. Connally always maintained three shots were fired: the first hit the president, the second hit Connally in the back, and the third struck Kennedy again. Kennedy was rushed to Parkland Hospital and pronounced dead soon after arrival. The bullet that tore through Connally's body was not fatal that day, but it was at least partially to blame for his death in 1993.

Connally recovered from his wounds and continued to serve Texas as its governor until he retired from the position in 1969. His administration was marked by his vigorous attempts to improve state education, even as the 1960s waves of unrest battered the rest of the country. Connally was popular in Texas as a rock-solid establishment candidate tied to the Kennedy tragedy in Dallas. He used his platform as governor to increase taxes substantially in order to finance higher salaries for teachers, better libraries, and research and new doctoral programs at state colleges. He also worked to establish a state fine arts commission and the University of Texas Institute of Texan Cultures, which was initiated as part of HemisFair '68, a state-supported world's fair in San Antonio.

Connally returned to the national political stage when President Richard Nixon named him secretary of the treasury in 1971. Connally switched political parties. He ran for office once more in 1980 when he sought the Republican nomination for the presidency, but withdrew after a disappointing showing in several state primaries.

He returned to the private sector and served either as a board member or a director for many corporations, including the Methodist Hospital of Houston, New York Central Railroad, Pan American Airways, the Andrew Mellon Foundation, the Greyhound Corporation, and Ford Motor Company. He was a member of the State Bar of Texas, and the American, Houston, and District of Columbia Bar Associations. He was also a partner in the law firm of Vinson, Elkins, Searls and Connally until 1985.

Long an advisor to entrepreneurs, Connally went into business for himself—along with former Lieutenant Governor Ben Barnes—in the 1980s. The company, which was involved in energy, land, and cattle speculation, experienced spectacular early success, but failed when the Texas economy crashed. Connally declared bankruptcy, and the former governor and his wife were forced to hold a public auction to sell their personal belongings. Many of their friends attended, bid generously, and returned all the purchased items to the Connallys.

Connally died in 1993 after a month-long struggle with pneumonia that doctors say was complicated due to the damage the assassin's bullet caused in 1963. At his funeral, Governor Ann Richards delivered one of the eulogies, summing up with the thought, "I lost a real good friend. . . . When important people die, you mourn the loss of their influence and their ability to get things done. All of that is true with John Connally, but it is harder for me to accept because of the fact that he was a personal friend."[10]

One of the Connallys' most treasured possessions now adorns the former governor's final resting place: a Victorian-era statue of St. Andrew sits atop a black marble obelisk-style marker in the Texas State Cemetery.

ANN WILLIS RICHARDS

1933–2006

REPUBLIC HILL, SECTION 2 (C2), ROW G, NUMBER 19

Giving John Connally a run for his money as the twentieth century's foremost Texas governor, Ann Richards had a reputation that reached far beyond the state's borders. Richards first gained national notoriety for her sense of humor at the 1988 Democratic Convention, upstaging Democratic presidential nominee Michael Dukakis with her famous speech declaring that George H. W. Bush had been born with "a silver foot in his mouth." She was a master of not only the one-liner, but also the stump speech and plain speech.

Richards's first elected office was to the Travis County Commission in 1976, and six years later, she became the first woman elected to a statewide office in Texas in more than fifty years when she became the state treasurer. Before that, Miriam "Ma" Ferguson had been the last woman to be elected to a statewide office. Richards and Ferguson could hardly have been more different as politicians. Ferguson ran under the slogan of "two governors for the price of one," implying her husband would run the governor's office as much as she did. Such a thought was anathema to Richards, who was outspoken, opinionated, and brought her own ideas to government. She is widely credited with modernizing the state treasurer's office and getting a return on the state's investment.

Richards, whose larger-than-life personality cast a shadow beyond the borders of Texas, was first asked to speak at the 1984 Democratic National Convention that nominated Walter Mondale. She was reelected treasurer in 1986 and was asked to speak again at the 1988 Democratic National Convention, this time delivering the keynote address.

Richard's frankness, sense of humor, and wit catapulted her to the elite level of the Texas Democratic Party, and, in 1990, she ran in the gubernatorial primary against former Governor Mark White and Attorney General Jim Mattox. The primary was vicious, including personal allegations against Richards by Mattox. *Texas Monthly* reporter Paul Burka said of the race, "I think the reason [Mattox] lost was that his campaign was over-the-top mean about Richards's personal life, including the drug allegations."[11] Richards won the primary, then went on to face Clayton Williams in the November general election.

Clayton Williams was the epitome of the Texas businessman and Richards stood in stark contrast to him. As noted writer and columnist Molly Ivins wrote, "Ann was the candidate of everybody else, especially women. She represented all of us who have lived with and learned to handle good 'ol boys, and she did it with laughter."[12]

Richards won the election and served four years as governor. One of her biggest accomplishments in that office was a reform of the prison system, which was overcrowded and ill equipped. Violent offenders were occasionally being released early to relieve crowding. During her term, twenty thousand beds were added to the prison system and a substance abuse program was established for offenders. She also presided over the legislature that passed the Texas Lottery and established the Lottery Commission. Richards herself bought the first lottery ticket in an Austin suburb. The lottery was pushed largely under the guise of school finance. Paying for Texas public schools has long been an

issue in the forefront of Texas taxpayers' minds. During Richards's term, the so-called Robin Hood Plan for school finance was launched. Under the plan, wealthier school districts sent money to poorer districts in an effort to level the playing field.

During her administration, Richards made the fledgling Texas film industry a priority. She said, "I've been a friend to Texas film since the number of people who cared about Texas film could have fit in a phone booth." She helped establish the Texas Film Hall of Fame and spoke often at the organization's annual functions. Richards's love of movies was well known and in what may have been her final public appearance, she filmed a short segment for the Alamo Drafthouse, a theater chain in Austin, imploring moviegoers to remain quiet during the film.

Richards called her administration the "New Texas," and she appointed more minorities and women to state boards and commissions than any previous governor. According to a *Houston Chronicle* article published upon her death, "about 44 percent of her appointees were female; 20 percent Hispanic; and 14 percent black.

When Richards left office in 1994 after her defeat by George W. Bush, she said, "I did not want my tombstone to read, 'She kept a really clean house.' I think I'd like them to remember me by saying, 'She opened government to everyone.'"[13] Bush was elected on the Republican tide that swept the country, but especially Texas. Richards had to find her way in a Republican-dominated political landscape. She did so by working privately on the national level, serving on many boards, including her service as a trustee of Brandeis University. She appeared on national talk shows, including *Larry King Live*, and her profile was generally higher nationally than in the state. She battled osteoporosis and coauthored the book *I'm Not Slowing Down: Winning My Battle With Osteoporosis*, with Dr. Richard Levine.

In 2006, she was diagnosed with esophageal cancer. Richards fought the disease for six months until she succumbed on September 13, 2006. Her private funeral at the Texas State Cemetery remains one of the largest funerals the Cemetery has yet seen. Richards now lies at rest beneath a hundred-year-old oak tree and next to her lifelong friend, journalist and author Bud Shrake.

BOB BULLOCK

1929–1999

REPUBLIC HILL, SECTION 1 (C1), ROW Q, PLOT 11

Not since Lyndon Johnson had Texas seen a public official who so many respected, feared, and loved. In the last thirty years of the twentieth century, no one dominated Texas politics like Bob Bullock. Johnson, Sam Rayburn, and John Nance Garner were major power brokers on the national level, but when it came to making state policy and legislation, it began and ended with Bullock. He loved Texas, and he signed off every speech with, "God bless Texas," a sentiment that can still be seen expressed on car bumper stickers across the state.

Bullock was born July 10, 1929, in Hillsboro, Texas. After graduating from Texas Tech University, he earned a law degree from Baylor University. But before he even graduated from law school, Bullock was well on his way to a political career: he was elected to the Texas House of Representatives in 1956. Three other freshman representatives elected at the same time—James Slider, Robert Johnson, and Byron Tunnell—became close friends and remained so until death parted them.

Bullock served in the House for two terms and then moved to Tyler to become a partner in Byron Tunnell's law practice. He returned to public life in 1969 when Preston Smith, whose campaign he had successfully managed, took office as governor. After the victory, Smith asked his campaign mastermind to be appoint-

ments secretary. Years later, when asked about the job, Bullock joked about its lack of excitement. "I appointed dead people," he said, ". . . even three convicted felons." When the secretary of state position became available, Smith appointed Bullock—the job was more eventful and a springboard to statewide power.

According to many Capitol insiders, a person quickly learned that it wasn't a good idea, or a pleasant option, to become Bullock's enemy. The politician had a long memory, which was borne out on the unusual occasions when he experienced defeat. Bullock had been appointed to the Insurance Commission, a position that required Senate confirmation. In a rare loss, Bullock was not confirmed. It was a slight that he would not allow himself to forget, or forgive. He kept the names of the senators who did not vote for him in his wallet for years so he could always remember who had voted against him.

Bullock was a great believer in government efficiency. When he was elected comptroller of public accounts in 1974, he discovered that the state's tax collecting agency was woefully outdated. He modernized the office by equipping it with computers, always pushing for better ways to improve government services. His ideas were controversial, but they also brought the comptroller's office into the age of technology.

As comptroller, Bullock's methods were sometimes

unorthodox: "Bullock's Raiders" would investigate a business that was delinquent on its tax bills and seize its assets, to be frozen until the bill was paid. Bullock summoned television crews to report on the businesses that weren't paying. Exposure on the six o'clock news proved to be an effective deterrent to tax delinquency. Modernization of the tax collecting agency brought in unprecedented revenue to the state.

His success as comptroller catapulted Bullock into the lieutenant governor's office in 1991. As lieutenant governor, usually considered the most powerful political position in the state, Bullock constantly looked for ways to improve government. One of his most clever political moves occurred after his first session. In 1991, Bullock aggressively attempted to reinvent Texas's outdated tax system and proposed a state income tax as a way to help the public school system. The income tax bill was unpopular, despised by the majority of Texans, and its passage could have ruined Bullock's career.

But Bullock sidestepped blame by pushing a constitutional amendment through the legislature that required that the people of Texas would have to vote to accept the state income tax. Bullock knew that such an eventuality would never come to pass, even though he had earmarked revenue from the tax to education. Thus, Bullock successfully turned the tide on this hot-button issue while still appearing to support the fiscally responsible expedient.

In 1994, the political landscape in the state began to change. With the election of George W. Bush as governor, the state turned from predominately Democratic to Republican. Before Bush, there had only been two Republican governors in the history of Texas, and one was a Reconstruction governor. Bush, despite growing up in a political family, had never held political office. But almost immediately, Bullock and Bush became allies. Partisanship, for Bullock, always took the back seat to what he thought was good for the state.

Bullock admired and respected the history of Texas. It is no surprise that after he attended the funeral of former House member Harry Whitworth in May 1994 at the Texas State Cemetery, he decided the Cemetery was in desperate need of improvements. The renovation of the Cemetery became Bullock's project, and he worked to get funding to make sure the down-and-out property would become a site that reflected the glory and history of the state.

The renovation lasted three years and was completed in 1997. A recirculating pond was added, the grounds were landscaped, thousands of headstones were cleaned, and a new Visitor Center was built. And, by a special request to Superintendent Harry Bradley, a flagpole—one hundred and fifty feet in height—was erected. The flagpole is the tallest in Travis County. Bullock wanted to be able to see the Cemetery from his office at the Capitol—the Texas flag fluttering from the pole is visible all the way to the Capitol across Interstate 35.

Never averse to controversy, Bullock crossed party lines in 1998 to endorse Governor Bush's reelection campaign. His loyalty was put to the test because Bush was running against Bullock's former personal assistant, Land Commissioner Gary Mauro. Bullock was widely criticized among Democratic Party loyalists, but he believed that Bush would best serve the interests of the state.

Many insiders believe that if Bullock had not taken a liking to the newly elected governor in 1994, Bush might never have gone further in his political career. From the beginning, the two had hit it off, and they became fast friends. Bullock and Bush worked together to make Bush's first gubernatorial term a success, which became a springboard to the Republican nomination for president. Bush had such respect for Bullock that he paid tribute to his mentor in his acceptance speech in July 2000: he ended with Bullock's trademark, "God Bless Texas" and then, "and God Bless Bob Bullock."

Bullock died June 18, 1999, and was buried on a rain-soaked Father's Day next to General Edward Burleson, the first person buried at the Texas State Cemetery.

Bullock will be remembered for both the positive and negative. He was devoted to moving Texas into the twenty-first century and to leaving the state better off than when it entered the twentieth century. Two lines on his headstone sum up what it meant to him to be a Texan and to devote more than forty years to public service: "God Bless Texas" and "Only Death will end my love affair with Texas." The administrative building at the Cemetery is named in his honor.

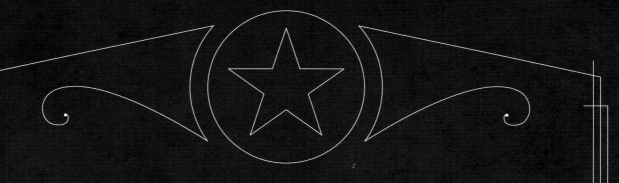

CHAPTER FIVE

CULTURAL ★ FIGURES

INTRODUCTION BY STEPHEN HARRIGAN

WILLIE JAMES
"EL DIABLO"

Willie James Wells
"El Diablo"

Played and managed in the Negro Leagues, 1924-1948. Began his career with the St. Louis Stars and became baseball's first power hitting shortstop. He was an eight-time all star for the Stars and teams in Chicago and Newark. Also, Wells starred in Canada, Cuba, Mexico, and Puerto Rico. He was inducted into the Cuban and Mexican Halls of Fame. He was best known for his aggressive play. During his career he compiled a .392 batting average against Major League ballplayers. In 1997, Willie Wells was inducted into the National Baseball Hall of Fame, in Cooperstown, New York, joining other Negro League greats.

AUGUST 10, 1906
JANUARY 22, 1989

WELLS

VIOLA GAY
BARNES
JAN. 11, 1902 – MAR. 7, 1999

VIOLA'S FATHER, ERNEST ROBERT BARNES
WAS THE CARETAKER OF THE BELL'S
STATE CEMETERY FROM 1912 TO 1950.
A NATIVE TEXAN, VIOLA ALONG WITH
HER SIBLINGS, LOVINGLY CARED FOR
THESE GROUNDS FOR 38 YEARS. SHE
MAINTAINED A LIFE-LONG INTEREST IN
THE WELFARE OF THE CEMETERY,
PROVIDING ANECDOTES AND PHOTOGRAPHIC
RECORDS DOCUMENTING ITS HISTORICAL
LEGACY. HER FONDEST MEMORIES WERE
THOSE SPENT HERE ON THESE SACRED
GROUNDS. SHE WAS A HUMBLE WOMAN
WHO LOVED ALL OF GOD'S CREATION,
ESPECIALLY CHILDREN, FLOWERS, AND
ANIMALS. VIOLA NEVER MARRIED, BUT
CHOSE INSTEAD TO INVEST HER LIFE IN
SERVING AND CARING FOR OTHERS.

ERNESTINE "DINK"
FORTENBERRY
JAN. 27, 1923

A FIRST LADY OF
WEST TEXAS

Grave of Willie James "El Diablo" Wells. Wells, a member of the National Baseball Hall of Fame in Cooperstown, New York, managed and played baseball in the Negro League from 1924 to 1948. Wells is considered the first power-hitting shortstop in baseball history. Wells died in 1989 and was reinterred at the Cemetery in 2004. Photograph by Laurence Parent.

INTRODUCTION

BY STEPHEN HARRIGAN

Stephen Harrigan is a novelist, journalist, and screenwriter. His novel The Gates of the Alamo *received numerous awards and was a New York* Times *best seller. Mr. Harrigan moved to Texas at the age of five. He graduated from the University of Texas at Austin in 1971.*

"I have come to value liberated minds as the supreme good of life on earth."

That is the testament carved into the back of the tombstone marking J. Frank Dobie's grave in the Texas State Cemetery. Dobie, the folklorist and essayist who had a long, lonely run as the symbol of Texas intellectual life, is buried alongside his wife, Bertha, in Section 1, Row F, Plot 23 on Republic Hill, just a few steps away from his great friend and fellow liberated mind, the historian Walter Prescott Webb. Liberated minds, though, when judged by the merciless ongoing attitudes of the living, are no more impervious to the corruptions of time than mortal bodies. Webb, for instance, has been attacked in recent years for a perception of God-given Anglo-Saxon superiority that runs through his pages. And perhaps Bertha McKee Dobie, if she were alive and attuned to the thinking of contemporary women, would be a bit annoyed to read the testimonial on the tombstone she shares with her famous husband: "She Was Ever Loyal."

Nevertheless, Dobie, Webb, and the other non-soldiers and non-statesmen (like Fred Gipson, James A. Michener, and Tom Landry) commemorated on Republic Hill represent enduring benchmarks of Texas culture, high and low and in-between. For pilgrims seeking the graves of intellectual titans, there are surely other places in the world to visit first. Paris's Pere Lachaise Cemetery features the resting places of Honoré de Balzac and Edith Piaf and Jim Morrison. Dostoyevsky and Tchaikovsky are interred in the Tikhvin Cemetery in St. Petersburg, and Poets Corner in Westminster Abbey houses the bones of Chaucer and Dickens. At the Texas State Cemetery, you can't aim much higher than the grave of the author of *Old Yeller*.

But it's poignant and peculiarly inspiring to stroll through the rows on Republic Hill and to see how these embattled intellectuals have been shoehorned in among the real movers and shakers of Texas history. Dobie, Webb, and Gipson are only a few yards downslope from Pompeo Coppini's towering statue of Stephen F. Austin, and their gravesites offer a commanding view of Elisabet Ney's sculpture of General Albert Sidney Johnston lying in knightly repose, with the white headstones of the Confederate dead fanning out beyond him. From Bigfoot Wallace to Ma Ferguson to Bob Bullock, the warriors, deal makers, legislators, and railroad commissioners of Texas still outrank and outnumber its writers, musicians, and painters.

That will inevitably change as Texas changes, as its molten history continues to cool. There will be more and more liberated minds for the grass in the Texas State Cemetery to grow over, and possibly in time even a few gravesites of such sacramental weight (Willie Nelson? Lance Armstrong?) that they rival anything in Pere Lachaise. But it would be a shame in a way if the balance ever really tipped, if the dreamers in the Texas State Cemetery outnumbered the doers. I doubt that even J. Frank Dobie, for all his rarefied sentiments, would really prefer to be surrounded by the like-minded dead. After all, without all those other folks lying under those other tombstones, without all the violence, heroism, bigotry, backroom dealing, and sometimes surprising reach of those splendidly unliberated minds, the chroniclers of Texas would have nothing to write about.

★

1888 JAMES FRANK
STORYTELLER OF THE S
PRESIDENTIAL MEDAL O

HIS WIFE
1890 BERTHA McKEE
SHE WAS EVER LO

OBIE 1964
THWEST
REEDOM

OBIE 1974

Will Erwin

Laurence Parent

LEA

TOM

BORN JULY 11, 1907 ✤ EL PASO, TX
DIED JAN. 29, 2001 ✤ EL PASO, TX

SARAH

BORN JAN. 6, 1912 ✤ MONTICELLO, IL

Sarah and I live on the east side of our mountain.
It is the sunrise side, not the sunset side.
It is the side to see the day that is coming,
not the side to see the day that is gone.
The best day is the day coming,
with the work to do,
with the eyes wide open,
with the heart
grateful.

In 1997, the Texas Legislature established new guidelines for burial in the State Cemetery. They included individuals who have contributed significantly to Texas culture, setting out nineteen categories ranging from arts and entertainment to business and financial contributions. Since these new guidelines were created, several notable Texans have been accepted for burial at the Cemetery. Prior to 1997, non—public officials had to get a governor's proclamation or a Senate concurrent resolution to be buried here.

JAMES FRANK DOBIE

1888–1964

REPUBLIC HILL, SECTION 1 (C1), ROW F, PLOT 23

James Frank Dobie was universally acknowledged as the "Storyteller of the Southwest." Shortly before his death, he was awarded the Presidential Medal of Freedom, the highest civilian honor that can be bestowed by the US government, by President Lyndon B. Johnson. When Dobie died on September 18, 1964, his funeral, held at the University of Texas's Hogg Auditorium, was followed by his burial at the Texas State Cemetery.

Dobie's death prompted special editions of both the *Austin American-Statesman* and the *Texas Observer* that featured tributes from his many fans. The outpouring of respect was the culmination of a sometimes controversial and always entertaining career.

Dobie, author of *The Longhorns*, a seminal work on the Southwest, was one of Texas's most prolific authors. Dobie said he wanted to "restore the flavor and gusto" to American literature, which he attempted with great flare. He was also an indefatigable critic of many institutions considered sacred in this state, including the University of Texas and statehouse politics. Even Texans in general didn't escape his notice.

The entry by Francis Edward Abernathy on J. Frank Dobie in the *Handbook of Texas* characterizes Dobie's worldview: "His war against bragging Texans, political, social and religious restraints on individual liberty, and the mechanized world's erosion of the human spirit was continual."[1]

Dobie was born on September 26, 1888, and raised on a ranch in rural Live Oak County. The ranch upbringing influenced his writing. Even at a young age, Dobie loved to read, and his parents encouraged his passion for literature with a steady stream of mail-order books. His fundamentalist father read to Frank and his five siblings from the Bible; his mother entertained them with readings from *Ivanhoe*, *Swiss Family Robinson*, and *The Pilgrim's Progress*.

At sixteen, Dobie left the ranch and moved to Alice to live with his grandparents and to finish high school. He went to college at Southwestern University in Georgetown, where he met Bertha McKee. After graduating in 1906, Dobie worked for newspapers and taught high school. But he wanted to write, and so Dobie left Texas in 1913 for the first prolonged period in

James Frank Dobie, author and University of Texas professor, was known as the "Storyteller of the Southwest." Photograph, titled "James Frank Dobie at Joe Small's Barbecue, ca. 1957," used with permission from the Prints and Photographs Collection, Dobie, J. Frank, file CN 03126, Briscoe Center for American History, University of Texas at Austin.

his life and enrolled in a graduate program at Columbia University in New York.

Dobie appreciated college life, but always said that New York City gave him a different sort of education. He spent days on end at the Metropolitan Museum of Art and took in performances of Shakespeare's plays. He later wrote that he "received more from New York theaters than from Columbia professors."

Dobie earned his master's degree at Columbia and returned to Texas in 1914 to join the faculty at the University of Texas. He also became a member of the Texas Folklore Society. The Society, founded in 1909 with a mission of preserving and presenting Texas folklore, was to become one of Dobie's passions.

Dobie married Bertha McKee in 1916 and left university life in 1917 to serve in World War I in a field artillery unit. His outfit was sent overseas near the end of the war, and Dobie was discharged in 1919. Later that same year, he returned to the University of Texas and published his first articles. It was not long before he became disenchanted with university life altogether and resigned his position to help manage his uncle Jim Dobie's Los Olmos ranch. His stay at the ranch was brief, but it was during that time that Dobie began to feel compelled to write about the history and folklore of the Southwest way of life.

In 1921, Dobie returned to the University of Texas and the Folklore Society, and three years later, he published his first book, *Legends of Texas*, a collection of stories about long-lost gold and silver mines and buried treasure around the state.

The book was a success, but that didn't guarantee success at the university. With only a master's degree in hand, Dobie was unable to get a promotion. A doctorate was mandatory. So Dobie decided to go where traditional credentials weren't so revered. Oklahoma A&M University (now Oklahoma State University) offered Dobie the chairmanship of the English department, and he accepted. He stayed at Oklahoma A&M from 1923 to 1925, returning to Austin and the University of Texas in 1925, enticed by the offer of a token promotion.

Dobie continued to write as well as to teach, and his second book, *Coronado's Children*, won the National Literary Guild Award in 1931. The book gave him national prominence, and he wrote several more during the 1930s, including *On the Open Range* (1931), *Tales of the Mustang* (1936), *The Flavor of Texas* (1936), and *Apache Gold and Yaqui Silver* (1939). Before World War II, Dobie published one more work—*The Longhorns*—and then set out on a sabbatical in Europe.

Dobie taught American literature at Cambridge University in England during the war and at universities in Germany and Austria after the war. He published a work based on his experiences called *A Texan in England*. Cambridge, he said, broadened his perspective and was the beginning of his acceptance of civilization, one where individuality was respected.

However, a broadened perspective wasn't what state government officials in Texas appreciated at the time. They became more and more critical of the liberal voices at the University of Texas and fired many professors they considered outspoken. Finally, in 1944, the Board of Regents fired university president Homer Rainey for what they viewed as his leftward leanings. Dobie—and a number of other professors—attacked the dismissal and in return, Governor Coke Stevenson called for Dobie's removal, labeling the writer a "troublemaker."

Stevenson was successful, thanks to a little-used rule that came to be known thereafter as the "Dobie Rule." Dobie had requested an extended leave of absence to remain in Europe, but the University had a two-year limit on sabbaticals—which Dobie had exceeded. Under this rule, Dobie and the University of Texas were divorced. Dobie's now-famous rebuttal was: "When I get ready to explain homemade fascism in America, I can take my example from the State Capitol of Texas."

Dobie continued to write after his termination. He produced eight more books between 1949 and 1964, the year of his death. After his death, his wife, Bertha, worked to publish his last two books, *The Cowpeople* and *The Rattlesnakes*.

Dobie's grave rests near two other prominent Texas authors, Fred Gipson and Walter Prescott Webb, in the shadow of Stephen F. Austin's grave on Republic Hill. Bertha Dobie, an accomplished author in her own right, died on December 18, 1974, and was also buried at the Texas State Cemetery.

FRED GIPSON

1908–1973

REPUBLIC HILL, SECTION 2 (C2), ROW D, PLOT 2

Fred Gipson, author of *Hound-Dog Man* and *Old Yeller*, was born February 7, 1908, near Mason, Texas. As a youth, Gipson had many adventures, memorable even for a boy growing up in the hardscrabble hill country of Texas. These adventures served as the backdrop for many of his later literary works. Walter Prescott Webb once said about Gipson, "Mark Twain knew the mind of the Missouri boy on the Mississippi and Fred Gipson knows the mind of a country kid in the Texas hill country just as well."[2]

One tale that Gipson told on himself revealed his early entrepreneurial bent. Rattlesnakes were a popular commodity not only for their skin, but also for their venom, which was valuable as an antitoxin. The young Gipson believed this could be a lucrative endeavor and decided to catch a few rattlers.

The hill country is crawling with the vipers, and the boy managed to snag one of them. He took it home—to the great distress of his mother. Gipson's father misinterpreted the hysterical interaction between mother and snake and assumed his wife and child were in mortal danger. He struck the snake down with his hoe, leaving young Fred to suffer the wrath of his mother as well as the loss of his newly created enterprise, which to the boy seemed to be far worse than any damage the snake might have caused.

After high school, Gipson took a highway construction job and saved money for college. In 1933, he enrolled at the University of Texas, where he became a columnist for the school newspaper, the *Daily Texan*. His writing attracted the notice of one of his professors—

J. Frank Dobie—who was not impressed. He once commented that Gipson "should get the notion out of his head of writing for a living."[3] Despite Dobie's criticism—or it may just have been a kindly warning—Gipson persevered. He eventually entered a writing contest and won first prize. One of the judges was Dobie, who must have thought Gipson's skills had improved.

In 1937, Gipson took a job at the *Corpus Christi Caller-Times*. As a columnist for the paper, Gipson had free rein to write about whatever he wanted; no story or subject was out of bounds. It was a dream job, and Gipson felt lucky that his editors recognized the nature of his talents. One editor at the *Caller-Times* commented at the time that Gipson was not much of a reporter but was a great writer.

Eventually, Gipson was fired. The setback allowed him to devote his efforts to writing full time. At first, he earned his living composing pulp Western novels and short stories, many of which evolved from old-timers' tales Gipson had heard in his younger days. His first serious writing was published in *Collier's*, and it sold for what was at the time the princely sum of five hundred dollars.

Another story rooted in his childhood recollections marked the beginning of Gipson's popular success. His father had a friend, Charlie Sanders, who hunted, fished, and trapped to make ends meet. Sanders often took the young Gipson on these expeditions. Later, Gipson remembered him as "the best outdoorsmen in the county." But, in addition to hunting and fishing, Sanders spent many days spinning yarns and teaching

Fred Gipson, author of Hound Dog Man *and* Old Yeller, *died peacefully in his sleep at his ranch on August 14, 1973, and was interred at the Texas State Cemetery. Used with the permission of Texas State Library and Archives Commission, Archives and Information Services Division, 1975/70-2053.*

Gipson the finer points of how to trap a raccoon or use jackrabbit liver for catfish bait.

Gipson wrote "My Kind of Man," a tale based on Sanders, which sold to *Reader's Digest* for sixteen hundred dollars. The success of the story proved a harbinger of what was to come. "My Kind of Man" evolved into *Clipped Wings*, the story of a twelve-year-old boy, Cotton Kinney, on his first hunt with a cantankerous outdoorsman, Blackie Scantling. The title *Clipped Wings* was changed to *Hound-Dog Man*, and eventually the story was made into a movie.

During the 1950s, Texas experienced its worst drought since the Dust Bowl of the 1930s. Gipson too was in the midst of a drought—he was having a difficult time getting his work published. After investing all the proceeds from *Hound-Dog Man* into his ranch, he was in dire need of a successful project.

His family, friends, and colleagues all knew he had yet to write his version of the great American novel. He was still searching for the one story that could define his career. Gipson again reached back into his own experience, recalling a story from his childhood. While riding home on horseback one evening, Gipson's grandfather had been attacked by a wild dog. His own dog—young Fred's beloved companion—fought off the aggressor, but it turned out that the wild dog had rabies. The family dog also became infected, of course, and Gipson's grandfather knew he had no choice but to shoot the boy's canine friend.

It took Gipson fewer than ninety days to write *Big Yeller Dog*, as he originally called the heartbreaking tale of friendship between a young boy and his dog. The title was later shortened to *Old Yeller*. Gipson's agent, Maurice Crain, said, "A great many people besides boys for a long string of years to come are going to be mighty grateful to you, Fred, for having written this . . . and I can think of no reason they would ever stop selling." Crain predicted that Gipson's great-grandchildren would draw royalties on "the yeller dog."[4]

The success of *Old Yeller* led to a movie deal with Walt Disney. Gipson followed up with a sequel to *Old Yeller* called *Savage Sam*. He was at the height of his professional career, but personal tragedy loomed. His son, Mike, committed suicide, and not long after, Gipson and his wife divorced.

Gipson tried writing again, but he never again reached the pinnacle he had achieved with *Hound-Dog Man*, *Old Yeller*, and *Savage Sam*. He spent his remaining years at his Mason County ranch, where he died in his sleep on August 14, 1973.

Today Gipson is buried alongside his fellow Texas writers, Walter Prescott Webb and J. Frank Dobie, on Republic Hill at the Texas State Cemetery.

HIS BOOKS ARE HIS MONUMENT.

WILLIE "EL DIABLO" WELLS

1906–1989

STATESMAN'S MEADOW, SECTION 2, ROW G, PLOT 33

Buck O'Neil, the chairman of the Negro Leagues Museum in Kansas City and the first black coach in the major leagues, said of Willie Wells, "I saw Honus Wagner play. I saw Pop Lloyd play. I love to watch Ozzie Smith play. . . . And if I had to pick a shortstop for my team, it would be Willie Wells. . . . Great as Ozzie Smith is, old-timers in St. Louis who saw Willie play for the St. Louis Stars still haven't seen his equal."[5]

Wells was born in Austin, Texas, on August 10, 1906. He grew up playing sandlot baseball before joining the St. Louis Stars of the Negro National League in 1925. His first season was disappointing, and Wells spent the off-season learning to hit a curveball. The next year, he hit .379, and by 1939, Wells was considered one of the fiercest competitors in all of baseball.

Wells played shortstop for several teams, won several championships, and played in eight Negro League All-Star games. Because he was such an aggressive ballplayer, Wells was often the subject of "beanball" incidents. As a result, he became a pioneer in the use of a batting helmet. Wells made his own protective headgear by modifying construction hard hats or coal miner's hats. His ingenious solution to getting hit in the head by a pitch was not well received by opposing pitchers, who saw it as an unfair advantage. Unfortunately, Wells probably had more pitches aimed at his well-protected head as a result.

Wells's defensive technique was fearsome: when a base runner headed into second base on a double play, Wells aimed the ball at the runner's eyes. If the runner didn't duck or slide to avoid getting hit, he would live to regret it. Conversely, if a base runner tried to take the shortstop out on his way to second base, Wells retaliated with a hard tag across the face. The tag hurt in part because of the force of Wells's arm, but there was another reason: Wells was known to pad his glove with little pieces of brick or rocks. Runners would think twice about trying to "spike" him.

Wells played winter baseball in Cuba and California until he was recruited to play in Mexico in 1940. While in Mexico, his aggressive play earned him respect and popularity among the fans, who affectionately nicknamed him "El Diablo." Wells and many other Negro Leaguers enjoyed their time playing south of the border. As he described it:

Players on teams in the Mexican League live just like big leaguers. We have everything first class, plus the fact that people here are much more considerate than the American baseball fan. I mean that we are heroes here and not just ballplayers. One of the main reasons I came back to Mexico is because I've found freedom and democracy here, something I never found in the United States. I was branded a Negro in the States and had to act accordingly. Everything I did, including playing ball, was regulated by my color. Well, here in Mexico, I am a man. I can go as far in baseball as I am capable of going. I can live where I please and will encounter no restrictions of any kind because of my race. That also had a lot to do with my decision to return here.[6]

Willie "El Diablo" Wells, National Baseball Hall of Fame member and power-hitting shortstop, died in 1989 and was laid to rest in Evergreen Cemetery in Austin. However, in 2004, his remains were moved to the Texas State Cemetery in recognition of his national cultural significance. Wells was considered one of the best shortstops to play the game by Buck O'Neil, the first black coach in major league baseball. Photograph donated to the Texas State Cemetery by a member of Wells's family.

Willie "El Diablo" Wells. Photograph donated to the Texas State Cemetery by a member of Wells's family.

Although blacks were barred from playing in the American and National Leagues, they showcased their skills against the white professional players in exhibition games. Exhibitions were serious business to the black players, who knew these games offered them the chance to prove a point. According to Buck O'Neil, the Negro Leaguers would play much harder, stretching singles into doubles, doubles into triples, and triples into home runs. They knew they had an advantage because the white players couldn't afford to get hurt in these games and ruin their careers. Playing opposite the white baseball stars, Wells compiled a .392 average against some of the greatest big league pitchers of the day, including Bob Feller and Warren Spahn.

During Wells's time with the Newark Eagles, he was appointed player/manager. His success as a manager was not only confirmed by the number of championships his team won but also by his development of young talent. He took particular pride in the accomplishments of major league greats Monte Irvin, Larry Doby, Don Newcombe, and Ernie Banks, all pupils of Wells and former players on his teams.

Another future Hall of Famer influenced by Wells was Jackie Robinson. Robinson was not considered the best player in the Negro Leagues nor had he ever played shortstop, the position for which the Dodgers recruited him. But he had other qualities that drew the interest of Brooklyn Dodgers general manager Branch Rickey. The Negro Leaguers recognized that Robinson had to succeed if others were to get a chance. When the Dodgers realized what all the Negro Leaguers knew—that Robinson was not suited to the shortstop position—they moved him to second base. Robinson had never played second base either and had serious doubts that he could make the transition. Wells stepped in and tutored Robinson, and the rest is history.

Sadly, by the time Robinson and Larry Doby successfully integrated baseball, most of the legendary Negro Leaguers were past their prime and had missed their shot at playing in the big leagues. In 1948, at the age of 43, "El Diablo" hit .328 with Memphis and retired from baseball with a .363 lifetime batting average. He was inducted into the National Baseball Hall of Fame in Cooperstown, New York, in 1997.

Wells died eight years before he was enshrined with the all-time baseball greats. He was originally buried at Evergreen Cemetery in Austin, but in October 2004, the Texas State Cemetery Committee had his remains disinterred and moved to the Cemetery. The Committee dedicated a monument with a bronze plaque similar to the one that commemorates him at Cooperstown. Buck O'Neil was the keynote speaker and offered many colorful anecdotes about playing against Wells.

THOMAS WADE LANDRY

1924–2000

REPUBLIC HILL, SECTION 2 (C2), ROW P, PLOT 15

Perhaps the most recognizable icon in Texas football history is the figure of legendary Dallas Cowboys coach Tom Landry stalking the sidelines at Texas Stadium in his suit and fedora. To most Texans, Coach Landry exemplified professionalism, integrity, and innovation—and, above all else, Landry and the Cowboys personified excellence. When Landry passed away in February of 2000, an era passed in Texas sports and culture.

Thomas Wade Landry was born September 11, 1924, in Mission, Texas. During high school, Landry developed into a star athlete at Mission High School, where, as quarterback, he led the football team to the South Texas regional championship. Following his successful high school career, Landry accepted a football scholarship to the University of Texas at Austin.

In 1942, shortly after his eighteenth birthday, Landry interrupted his education to join the US Air Corps. During World War II, he flew thirty B-17 combat missions, experiencing several close calls. One of these occurred following a bombing run in Czechoslovakia. Flying above France, Landry realized his B-17 was running out of fuel, but weather conditions would not permit a safe landing. He circled, looking for alternative landing bases, but his plane began to drop and he crash-landed. Luckily, his crew escaped with just a few scratches; because the plane had been out of fuel, there was no explosion. Landry later said about his World War II service, "War had tested me, but I had survived. And that experience [gave] me not only a broader perspective on life, but a confidence in myself I had never known before."

Landry arrived back at the University of Texas in 1946 and became an all-conference fullback in the old Southwest Conference. Following the 1949 Orange Bowl, Landry's final game as a collegiate athlete, the New York (football) Yankees of the All-American Football Conference signed him to a professional contract for $6,000 with a $500 signing bonus. With a paying job, Landry could now marry his college sweetheart, Alicia Wiggs.

After only a year, the All-American Football Conference and the National Football League merged and Landry found himself playing defensive back for the New York Giants. He made All-Pro and was named an assistant coach while still playing for the Giants. While in New York, Landry honed his reputation as an innovator: he created the 4-3 defense, which became the predominant defense in the NFL and is still used as a base defense for the majority of NFL teams. Two Hall of Fame coaches called plays for the Giants: Landry was the defensive coordinator and Vince Lombardi was the offensive coordinator. Together they were the architects of the Giants' first NFL championship since 1938.

Following the 1958 season, Lombardi was hired first by the Green Bay Packers, and then, in 1959, Landry was hired by an upstart franchise in Dallas, the Cowboys. Landry and the Cowboys started slowly; six seasons passed before the team had a .500 record. But once the Cowboys started winning behind Don Meredith and Bob Lilly, they never looked back; under Landry, the team put together an unprecedented run of twenty straight winning seasons, five Super Bowl appearances, and two Super Bowl wins.

*Legendary Dallas Cowboys coach
Tom Landry on the sidelines
during a game. His trademark
hat is featured on his cenotaph at
the Texas State Cemetery. Image
provided by Alicia Landry.*

Always the innovator, Landry pioneered the flex and multiple defensive sets. His offenses were just as complex; using the skills of All-Pro quarterback Roger Staubach, Landry designed the "shotgun" or "spread" formation, multiple shifts, and "men in motion" to attempt to complicate and confuse the opponent's defensive sets. After inventing the 4-3 defense, he had gone on to invent an offense to beat it.

At the pinnacle of his career and the Cowboys' success, the Cowboys became known as "America's Team"—a label still used today. Landry noted, "The moment I heard it, I thought, 'Oh, no! Everybody's really gonna be gunnin' for us now.'" But the rest of the league knew the Cowboys had a mystique about them: one former NFL player said of the Cowboys, "You . . . always pull it out in the end." Landry would later embrace the title.

The late eighties were extremely difficult for Landry and the Cowboys; following a division championship in 1985, the Cowboys didn't have another winning season under Coach Landry. By 1989 the Cowboys had suffered their third straight losing season, and Landry left coaching, following the sale of the team to new owners. In his first year of eligibility, Landry was inducted into the Pro Football Hall of Fame in Canton, Ohio.

Tom Landry will always be remembered for his stoic demeanor, his professionalism on the sidelines, and his faith (he was active in the Fellowship of Christian Athletes even after he retired). His Cowboys became a cultural phenomenon, and in Texas, where football is a way of life, Landry became a legend. Still, his most lasting achievement will not be his greatness as a coach, but his greatness as a person.

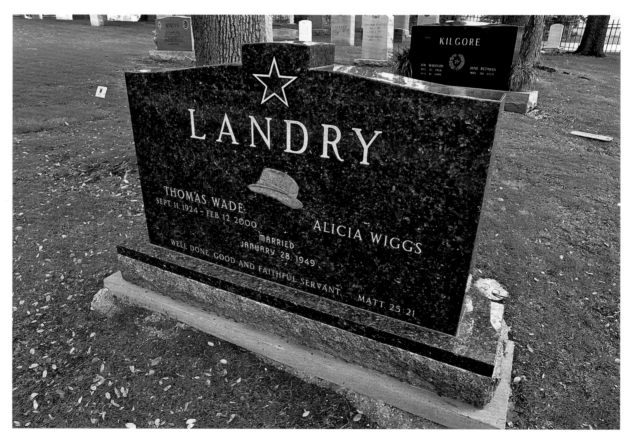

Cenotaph of Thomas Wade Landry, longtime coach of the Dallas Cowboys. Landry is buried in Dallas, but his memory is honored with a cenotaph at the State Cemetery for his place in Texas football history. Photograph by Laurence Parent.

THOMAS CALLOWAY LEA

1907–2001

Tom Lea's drawings and paintings evoked, and then came to define, the American Southwest. Romantic but also precise, his work represents the essence of a Texas now gone. Although Lea was known primarily as a painter of Western landscapes, he was also a muralist, an author, and a war correspondent for *Life* magazine. His portraits of Chiang Kai-shek and Madame Chiang Kai-shek are refined examples of the diversity of Lea's talent.

Lea was born July 11, 1907, in El Paso, where his father was a lawyer and mayor. Lea began drawing while still a toddler. Art was an all-consuming passion, and after he graduated from El Paso High School in 1924, he opted to attend the Art Institute of Chicago instead of pursuing a traditional education at a four-year liberal arts college. At the Art Institute, he studied with the well-known Chicago muralist John Norton.

During his second year there, Lea met and married fellow student Nancy Jean Taylor. After the couple graduated, they traveled to Italy to study Renaissance frescoes. Then in 1933, Lea and his wife moved to Santa Fe, where he completed several murals and paintings for the Works Progress Administration. Lea obtained another impressive commission in 1935: two murals for the Texas Centennial Celebration for the Hall of State at the State Fairgrounds in Dallas.

Lea returned home to El Paso in 1936 after his wife's death. There he met two people who were to become lifelong friends, as well as collaborators: publisher Carl Hertzog and J. Frank Dobie, with whom he worked for many years. Lea illustrated Dobie's book *Apache Gold and Yaqui Silver* and later illustrated *The Longhorns*.

When Lea became a novelist, Dobie praised his first book, *The Brave Bulls*, saying it was written with "the utmost of economy" and was "beautiful in its power."[7] In its spareness and power, Lea's writing was very much like his art. Perhaps the most vital memento of their relationship is the portrait Lea painted of Dobie not long before the folklorist died. Also rendered with the utmost economy, the now famous black-and-white profile of the writer is the likeness that has come to be most associated with Dobie.

In 1938, after a whirlwind, thirty-six-hour courtship, Sarah Dighton Beane became Lea's second wife. Theirs was a partnership that would last until his death, sixty-three years later.

In 1940 another long association began. *Life* magazine offered the artist a position as a correspondent. Lea's job was to visit military bases in anticipation of possible US involvement in World War II. He traveled far and wide in this job—from Fort Sam Houston in San Antonio to the South Pacific after Pearl Harbor.

Many of his paintings feature the daily lives of soldiers and are now on display at the US Army Center for Military History in Washington, DC. During the war, Lea landed with the first assault wave of the First Marines on the Pacific island of Peleliu on September 15, 1944. It was a bloody battle, and Lea's subsequent portrait of a soldier with a slack face and wide eyes—*The Two-Thousand-Yard Stare*—came to be his most famous war

representation. The painting also came to represent to the nation the shock of battle. Lea spent some of his time in China, where he painted Chinese nationalist leader Chiang Kai-shek and his wife. *Life* published Lea's works between 1941 and 1945.

After the war, *Life* assigned Lea to research and illustrate the historical aspects of the beef industry in the New World. Lea produced an illustrated pamphlet titled *A Bullfight Manual for Spectators*. It inspired his first novel, *The Brave Bull*, which was subsequently made into a movie. Lea wrote three more novels: *The Wonderful Country*, *The Primal Yoke*, and *The Hand of Cantu*. He continued to paint into the 1970s. One of his later paintings, *The Ranger Escort West of the Pecos*, hangs in the governor's business office at the Capitol in Austin.

Toward the end of his life, Lea received the Colonel John Thomason Award for excellence in art in depicting the Marine Corps. He was also given a lifetime achievement award by the Texas Institute of Letters and was named a Fellow of the Texas State Historical Association. The El Paso Museum of Art also dedicated a gallery in his name.

Tom Lea, artist and novelist, died January 21, 2001, in El Paso, where he is also buried. On May 14, 2005, Lea's friends and family attended a ceremony at the State Cemetery in Austin to commemorate his contributions to Texas and to the United States and to dedicate a cenotaph erected on the grounds of the Cemetery in his honor. Lea family friend Stephen W. Pogson wrote, "His family, friends, and fans placed a cenotaph, or memorial marker, in his honor in the Texas State Cemetery, where his name will now be remembered with his good friends, colleagues, and contemporaries like J. Frank Dobie, Walter Prescott Webb, Fred Gipson, and Buck Schiwetz."

The mahogany granite cenotaph features a mountain bearing a quote from Lea: "Sarah and I live on the east side of our mountain. It is the sunrise side, not the sunset side. It is the side to see the day that is coming, not the side to see the day that is gone. The best day is the day coming, with the work to do, with the eyes wide open, with the heart grateful."

Thomas Calloway Lea's Rio Grande, *oil on canvas, 22 × 32", painted in 1954. Image courtesy of El Paso Museum of Art, gift of Mr. and Mrs. Robert W. Decherd in honor of Isabelle Thomason Decherd and H. Ben Decherd.*

MAY PETERSON THOMPSON

1880–1952

REPUBLIC HILL, SECTION 1 (C1), ROW G, PLOT 18

May Peterson, dubbed the "Golden Girl of the Metropolitan Opera" by the New York media, married Ernest O. Thompson on June 9, 1924, in Bronxville, New York. The two first met in 1921, when Peterson traveled to Thompson's hometown of Amarillo to perform. At the time, Thompson was a young and ambitious lawyer, who later was mayor of Amarillo and served for thirty-two years on the Texas Railroad Commission.

May Peterson was born October 7, 1880, in Oshkosh, Wisconsin. Her father was a minister, and she grew up singing and playing the organ in church. She briefly studied singing at the Chicago Conservatory of Music, venturing on to Europe at the age of seventeen to continue her studies. She raised three hundred dollars for the trip by singing in choirs and performing in recitals.

While in Europe, Peterson gave English lessons and sang in American churches and clubs. But it was a life of hardship—she often had little to eat and not much money. But the singer was nothing if not determined, and she became well known in Europe for her coloratura soprano voice.

Her biggest break came when she was offered the title role in Jules Massenet's *Manon*—an opera both feared and loved by singers for its length and difficulty—in Vichy during a summer festival. Peterson's successful debut led to invitations to sing again in Vichy and in other venues along the French Riviera. She was also a favorite in pri-

vate concerts for some of Europe's most glamorous and distinguished leaders; it was rumored that she performed a pre–World War I concert for Kaiser Wilhelm.

Before the war broke out, Peterson again had the lead in *Manon* at Paris's Theatre Lyrique and the Opera Comique. But both opera houses closed during the war, so she moved to London where she sang at the Mozart Festival under Sir Henry Wood.

Following her stint in Europe, Peterson returned to the United States and began touring. The Metropolitan Opera signed her to perform in Giacomo Puccini's *La Bohème* and other operas. She also sang in recital at the Aeolian Hall and Carnegie Hall, in addition to having the distinction of being one of the first singers broadcast over the radio. Thomas Edison heard one of the radio broadcasts and was quoted as saying, "That is one of the finest lyric voices in the United States."

After her marriage to Thompson, Peterson joined her husband in Amarillo and gave up the opera, although she occasionally went on tour. When Thompson was appointed to the Texas Railroad Commission, the couple moved to Austin.

On October 1, 1952, May Peterson Thompson suffered a cerebral hemorrhage while vacationing at their summer home in Estes Park, Colorado. She was flown back to Austin and died there on her birthday, October 7, 1952. She was laid to rest at the Texas State Cemetery. Her husband died in 1966 and is buried next to her.

CHAPTER SIX

EDUCATORS

★

AND

★

ACADEMICS

INTRODUCTION BY DR. STEVEN WEINBERG

INTRODUCTION

BY DR. STEVEN WEINBERG

Dr. Steven Weinberg is a world-renowned physicist. In 1979, he won the Nobel Prize in Physics. He holds the Jack S. Josey-Welch Foundation Chair in Science at the University of Texas at Austin. Dr. Weinberg was educated at Cornell and Princeton. He joined the University of Texas faculty in 1982.

When settlers first came to Texas, they faced problems of opening land for agriculture, fighting Indians, and dealing with the terrible divisions marked by the Texas War of Independence and the Civil War—problems enough without worrying also about higher education. Even so, from the beginning, some Texans dreamed of building a civilized society, graced by colleges and universities. The first colleges, founded during the Republic, were small church schools: Southwestern in 1840 and Baylor and Mary Hardin Baylor in 1845. Trinity University (named after the river) was founded after the Civil War, in 1869.

None of these had endowments that could compare with those of schools like Harvard and Yale back east. Only the state itself had the resources to build a major university. The Republic had called for the foundation of a university "of the first class" and had set aside fifty leagues of land as an endowment, but never got around to actually founding a university. Gideon Lincecum, the first Texan to earn an international reputation in the sciences, was self-educated and never held a university position.

Finally, in the period 1876–1881, the state started to found universities: Texas A&M at College Station, Prairie View A&M, the University of Texas at Austin, and the UT Medical Branch at Galveston.

The pond winds throughout the Cemetery from the west side to the east side. It was added during the 1994–1997 renovations overseen by Bob Bullock. Photograph by Laurence Parent.

A view of the plaza at the south end of the Cemetery. The State Cemetery grounds crew oversees daily the planting of flowers, the care of grass, and the maintenance of plots. Photograph by Laurence Parent.

No one did more to bring this about than Ashbel Smith, a founding commissioner of Prairie View, a founding regent and first president of the University of Texas, and instigator of the Medical Branch.

Since then, the universities and colleges of Texas have grown gradually in strength and prestige. The University of Texas at Austin, Texas A&M University at College Station, and Rice University are now internationally recognized centers of research; the University of Texas medical schools and Baylor College of Medicine are among the world's best; and there are pockets of excellence in numerous other Texas schools.

This growth of higher education both affected and was affected by the public life of Texas. Page Keeton, the long-serving dean of the University of Texas School of Law, staunchly defended academic freedom in the 1950s and 1960s and followed both the letter and the spirit of the Supreme Court decision that opened the law school to black students.

Despite the growth of Texas higher education, scholars and scientists are thin on the ground (or perhaps one should say, under the ground) in the Texas State Cemetery. This is in part because for many years eligibility was generally limited to Civil War veterans, elected state officials, members of state commissions, and their spouses. It took a governor's proclamation or legislative action to open the Cemetery to Frank Dobie or Page Keeton. In 1997, the legislature created the Texas State Cemetery Committee, which can admit Texans who have made a significant contribution to our state in any line of work. Educators will probably not have gravestones that can stand comparison with the monuments to Stephen F. Austin or Albert Sidney Johnston, but they will at least be present in increasing numbers, giving silent evidence that science and scholarship flourish in Texas.

★

There are many educators buried at the Cemetery. Several—for example, J. Frank Dobie and Barbara Jordan—are featured in this book, in other sections. Some profiled in this section are not educators in the true sense, but they did significantly contribute to Texas education.

ASHBEL SMITH

1805–1886

REPUBLIC HILL, SECTION 1 (C1), ROW Q, PLOT 15

Ashbel Smith was Texas's first Renaissance man. Smith indefatigably assumed the roles of linguist, scientist, physician, editor, writer, farmer, rancher, philosopher, soldier, diplomat, statesman, and educator. He contributed much to Texas, but his most lasting contributions were in medicine and education, and he is referred to as both the "Father of Texas Medicine" and the "Father of the University of Texas."

Smith was born on August 13, 1805, in Hartford, Connecticut, to Moses Smith Jr. and Phoebe Adams Smith. In 1823, he enrolled at Yale. Following his graduation, he taught school in North Carolina before deciding to study medicine. He earned his MD and worked for a short period at the Retreat for the Insane in Hartford. But Smith was impatient, and he wanted to see the world: he left for North Carolina to set up a private practice and then moved to Paris in 1832 to further his studies in medicine.

While in Paris, Smith took advantage of every opportunity to study under the most prominent physicians in the world. He honed his medical skills and published articles, including one on cholera. He also joined in the Paris social whirl, mingling with the likes of Samuel Morse and the legendary French General Lafayette. Eventually, though, Smith returned to North Carolina to resume private practice. He was to return again, however, to Paris, a city that had captured his imagination.

Smith did not stay long in North Carolina. He traveled to the southeastern United States, stopping in New Orleans. While there, he met James Pinckney Henderson, who was recruiting troops for the Texas army. Henderson offered Smith the position of surgeon general. Smith demurred, until Henderson mentioned a possible diplomatic position in France. Upon his arrival in Texas, Smith befriended Sam Houston; the two became close friends and remained confidants throughout their Texas careers.

As surgeon general in the Texas army, Smith implemented new administrative policies, such as an organizational chart for each Texas division and a board of examiners to oversee the license applications of new physicians. Smith and other physicians organized the Medical and Surgical Society of Galveston, which was to create a set of standards for Texas doctors, to promote training, to establish a network for sharing ideas, and to control the licensing of new doctors in Texas. The organization would eventually become the Texas Medical Association.

Ashbel Smith, called the "Father of the University of Texas" and the "Father of Texas Medicine," died in 1886 at his plantation, Evergreen, on Galveston Bay and was buried at the Texas State Cemetery. Photograph used with the permission of Texas State Library and Archives Commission, Archives and Information Services Division, 1/102-521.

IN MEMORY OF

PIONEER PATRIOT

AND

STATESMAN

ASHBEL SMITH

Came to Harris County, Texas in 1837
from Connecticut, and soon thereafter
appointed Surgeon General in the Army
of the Republic. Minister to France 1842 - 5
Joined Gen. Taylors Army in 1846 in its march
upon Mexico. Was Colonel of the 2nd Texas
Infantry in Confederate Army. Served in the
Texas Legislature in 1866. In 1878 was
Commissioner from Texas to the Paris
Exposition. Member University Board of
Regents 1881 to his Death.

Born at Hartford, Conn. August 13, 1805
Died Jan. 21, 1886

Smith was an effective administrator as well as a skilled physician—and he proved to be just as competent politically. The fact that he managed both to support Sam Houston's archrival Mirabeau B. Lamar for president of Texas in 1838 and to maintain his friendship with Houston proved that the doctor was astute, if not the ultimate diplomat.

Following the annexation of Texas by the United States, Smith committed himself to developing an educational system in the state. After a seizure left him temporarily incapacitated, he returned to Connecticut to recover. While convalescing, he examined literature and textbooks to be used in Texas schools, and later, when he returned to Texas, he lobbied the legislature to create a state school commission, which set up a fair and equitable public school system.

The Civil War intervened and forced Smith to leave behind his work on education. Smith was committed to states' rights and decided to fight for the cause. He formed the Bayland Guards, a regiment that was mustered into service as the Second Texas Infantry. The regiment fought in the Battle of Shiloh, where Smith was wounded. He recovered from his wounds and returned to his company, which was assigned to defend Vicksburg in a siege that began on May 22, 1863, and dragged on until July 4, 1863. Confederate General James Pemberton surrendered after the forty-day struggle; Ashbel Smith and his men were captured but were later paroled and sent home.

Following the war, Smith was elected to the Eleventh Texas Legislature in 1866, but found his opposing views, which were unpopular, a hindrance to productivity. During this time, Smith was asked to oversee the removal of General Albert Sidney Johnston's body from New Orleans to be reinterred at the Texas State Cemetery.

Texas education and medicine continued to be Smith's two main causes. He was at the forefront in advancing the idea that the state needed a medical school, but he was also an ardent supporter of educating former slaves. The legislature named him one of the three commissioners in the newly formed "Agricultural and Mechanical College of Texas, for the benefit of the Colored Youths." The school was located in Prairie View; the official name was later changed to Prairie View State Normal School. Today it is known as Prairie View A&M.

In 1881, the legislature established the University of Texas and recognized the doctor's commitment to education by appointing Smith to the first board of regents. The board promptly elected him president and then tackled the task of creating a master plan for the university. Smith, the consummate organizer and catalyst, created plans for curriculum, faculty guidelines, blueprints for buildings, and the overall direction and mission of the university. But perhaps his biggest battle was the fight for the location of the school's medical branch. Smith preferred Galveston, at the Texas Medical College and Hospital, and he got his way.

Smith died January 21, 1886, at his plantation, Evergreen, on Galveston Bay and was buried at the Texas State Cemetery.

GIDEON LINCECUM

1793–1874

REPUBLIC HILL, SECTION 1 (C1), ROW V, PLOT 3

Gideon Lincecum was a self-taught naturalist, a practicing botanical physician, and a regular correspondent with Charles Darwin, Alexander von Humboldt, Louis Agassiz, and other great naturalists in the United States and abroad. His work chronicling the ecology of Texas was—and still is—internationally known and respected, and even today his papers are a unique and impressive compendium of flora and fauna from a time long gone.

Lincecum was a member of and contributed papers to numerous scientific societies, notably the Smithsonian Institution, the Franklin Institute, and the Essex Institute, to which he also gave a collection representing forty-eight different families of ants and butterflies. He sent specimens of all the flora of Texas to the *Jardin des Plantes* in Paris, and his monograph on the Texas red ant—the study to which he devoted fourteen years—remains pertinent today. Lincecum's work did not stop at ecology, though; he also delivered anthropological studies of several Indian tribes.

Lincecum was born April 22, 1793, in Warren County, Georgia, to Hezekiah and Sally Lincecum. He spent most of his early life in the southeastern United States before settling in Mississippi. Lincecum was one of the early settlers of Monroe County, Mississippi, where he was an entrepreneur, a county judge, and the postmaster. A believer in the education of children, he was one of the co-founders of the Franklin School, the first free school in Mississippi.

One of Lincecum's most significant contributions to education was his publication of "Chahta (Choctaw) Tradition," a detailed account of an aging Choctaw warrior, who spoke of the origins of the Choctaw and their relationship with the European settlers. The work also describes the Choctaw building methods, farming techniques, and spiritual beliefs and is considered to be one of the definitive pieces of scholarship on the Choctaw nation. In addition to "Chahta Tradition," Lincecum wrote a biography on the Choctaw leader Apushimatah, which gave a historian's insight into the hierarchy of the Choctaw Nation and the eventual removal of the Choctaw to Oklahoma.

By 1848, Lincecum had acquired enough financial security as a physician to move his family to present-day Washington County, Texas. There, he devoted much of his time to his naturalist interests. Fascinated by the ant, he wrote several papers about ant behavior, which he submitted to Charles Darwin. Darwin, impressed by the amateur naturalist, presented Lincecum's paper to the *Journal of the Linnaean Society of London*, which represented the thinking of the European scientific elite.

Lincecum was a die-hard Confederate and an avid believer in states' rights. Devastated by the outcome of the Civil War, he left the United States and moved to Tuxpan, a colony of Confederates in Mexico. Lincecum lived in Mexico for six years, working and searching out new plants and animals.

Lincecum returned to Texas, where he died November 28, 1874, at his Long Point home. He was buried at Mount Zion Cemetery near Burton, and his remains were moved to the Texas State Cemetery in 1937.

Without a formal education, Lincecum was a competent physician, botanist, naturalist, anthropologist, and writer.

WERDNER PAGE "DEAN" KEETON

1909–1999

REPUBLIC HILL, SECTION 1 (C1), ROW E, PLOT 3

P age Keeton was the dean of the University of Texas School of Law for more than a quarter of a century—so long, in fact, that people simply referred to him as "Dean Keeton."

Werdner Page Keeton was born August 22, 1909, in McCoy, Texas. He graduated from high school at fifteen and the next year he enrolled in the three-year pre-law program at the University of Texas. In 1928 he entered the University of Texas School of Law and graduated in 1931.

After a brief stint practicing law in Vernon, Texas, Keeton was invited back to the University of Texas to work as a research assistant. A year later—at the age of twenty-three—Keeton was appointed to an assistant professorship. He taught for three years and then took a sabbatical to begin graduate studies at Harvard University School of Law. His work was impressive, and after completing his studies, Keeton was offered several teaching positions at Harvard. He declined them all because he wanted to return to the University of Texas.

By 1940, Keeton was assistant dean of the School of Law. When World War II broke out, he sought an officer's commission, but his poor eyesight and high blood pressure were disqualifications. Instead, he went to work in Washington for the Office of Price Administration and later the Petroleum Administration for War, where he administered the program for setting oil and gas prices. His experience during World War II brought several lucrative job offers from the oil and gas industry, which Keeton declined in favor of returning to his beloved University of Texas. He later said of his time during World War II, "Except for my experiences as a legal educator and scholar, I have always regarded my experience as a lawyer with the war agencies in Washington, DC, during World War II as the most valuable of my career."[1]

Keeton did venture once from academic life in Texas. A year after his return from Washington, Keeton accepted the deanship at the school of law at the University of Oklahoma. His blood still ran pure burnt orange, but he was, as always, thinking ahead. "The University of Oklahoma wasn't nearly as good as this [University of Texas] law school," he said, "but I wanted to experience running a law school."[2]

This proved a wise choice. In 1949 Keeton returned to the University of Texas as dean of the law school. But he was thrown into the vortex of controversy almost immediately. In 1950, the Supreme Court announced one of the landmark civil rights decisions, and it involved the University of Texas: *Sweatt v. Painter* ruled that a "good faith" effort by states to ensure a separate but equal education was no longer good enough. Now states had to assure true equality in providing educational opportunities to blacks. As a result of the ruling, Heman Marion Sweatt was admitted to the university's law school. There were student groups, parents, and alumni who objected to Sweatt's enrollment. But Dean Keeton was adamant. He adhered to the Supreme Court decision, and Heman Sweatt was enrolled in the law school peacefully.

The political climate of the 1950s and 1960s was tumultuous, and Keeton adroitly guided his school

through the rough waters. At one point, the University of Texas Board of Regents ordered Keeton to provide them with a list of the law school faculty members with their political leanings noted. The regents wanted to know who was conservative, who was liberal, and who, if anyone, was in between. Astounded by their disregard for the importance of diverse ideas in a faculty, Keeton snapped back in a letter: "We appoint people over here on the basis of their ability—competence to teach and write."[3]

Keeton sidestepped a showdown with the administration, but the issue reared its head again several years later, in the mid-1960s, when the administration questioned the "radical" ideology of some members of the law school faculty. This time, the board of regents had a heavier club to wield: it froze the law school's budget at the previous year's level. Keeton expressed disappointment at the administration's attempt to control the hiring process and took measures to thwart the challenge to academic freedom. He took the fight outside the confines of the campus, rallying his alumni base.

Keeton referred to the reputation of the law school in speeches he delivered throughout the year. Using the school's reputation as his rallying point, Keeton said, "We have a faculty—carefully selected without reference to race, religion, or political philosophy—of diverse viewpoints. If it were not so, we would be subject to criticism, because our students should be subjected to a competition of ideas."[4] The integrity and reputation of the law school were being impugned, and the alumni let their opinions be known. The board of regents backed down.

Keeton considered the creation of the University of Texas Law School Foundation to be his greatest contribution to the law school. At the time, it too was controversial. Outside fund-raising efforts are now the norm at universities, but in 1952, the concept seemed revolutionary. The key, as Keeton saw it, was to appoint a fund-raising board powerful enough that it could not "be brushed aside." Keeton's defense of the formation of the Foundation was powerful and simple, "Look, it's better to have money and problems than no money."

Keeton not only served as dean of the law school but also sat on several boards and commissions. He was a member of President Lyndon B. Johnson's Labor Management Policy Committee, chairman of the State Bar of Texas Penal Code Revision Advisory Committee, and a consultant to the US Senate Committee on Commerce, Science, and Transportation, among many others.

In 1974, Governor Dolph Briscoe proclaimed Dean Keeton eligible for burial in the Texas State Cemetery. The Briscoe proclamation stated, "Whereas, as Professor of Law and for twenty-five years Dean of the School of Law of the University of Texas, and as a member of many State Bar of Texas committees and Legislative Study Commissions created for the purpose of improving the administration of the law and of justice, Werdner Page Keeton has rendered unusually distinguished service to the people of Texas."

In 1995, Twenty-sixth Street, which borders one side of the School of Law, was renamed Dean Keeton Street in honor of his service to the University of Texas. Keeton died January 10, 1999, and was buried at the Texas State Cemetery. Keeton's daughter, Carole Keeton Strayhorn, who has held elected positions in both the city of Austin and state government, recalled one of her father's remarks that came to be the greatest lesson in her life: "It's not the dollars you make that matter. It's the difference you make."

WALTER PRESCOTT WEBB

1888–1963

Movies, television shows, books, and magazine and newspaper articles have chronicled the history and the colorful characters that personify the legend behind the Texas Rangers, one of the most storied law enforcement agencies in the world. The legend of the Texas Rangers began during the Texas War for Independence and has continued to grow over the years. But there was more to the legend than just hearsay and tall tales—much of what made the Rangers legendary was the truth.

Walter Prescott Webb, a history professor at the University of Texas during the 1930s, '40s, and '50s, was one of the country's premier historians. Fascinated by the Texas Rangers since his days in graduate school, he had even written his master's thesis on the topic. That work eventually became a book: *The Texas Rangers: A Century of Frontier Defense*. Published in 1935, it was the definitive book on the beginnings of the famed law enforcement agency. The Rangers admired Webb and the book and showed their appreciation by making him an honorary Texas Ranger in 1935.

Webb was born on April 3, 1888, in Panola County, Texas. His family moved west to Stephens County, where his father was a teacher and a part-time farmer. Webb attended school in Ranger and graduated from Ranger High School. He then earned a teaching certificate. But his education had already taken a fortuitous turn.

As a boy, Webb found farm life to be harsh and yearned for something more. He was an avid reader and, in desperation, wrote to the Confederate magazine *Sunny South*, asking for advice on the best way for a farm boy to earn an education. The letter was published in the magazine and had an effect on one of its readers. William Hinds, a wealthy New York businessman, who ran a novelty goods business, wrote to Webb and offered to send books and magazines to the young Texas reader. Each Christmas, Hinds also sent the young farm boy an expensive designer tie from New York, which Webb wore with pride.

After Webb began teaching, Hinds—with whom Webb still corresponded—inquired about the young man's plans and offered his help. With Hinds's financial assistance, Webb enrolled at the University of Texas at Austin. He graduated in 1915 at the age of twenty-seven. Hinds died the next year. Webb never met his benefactor and was unable to repay him, but he decided the best way to show his gratitude was to do the same for other children in financial need.

After graduating from UT, Webb taught high school for a year before he was offered a position in the history department at the university. As he was beginning work on his master's degree at the University of Texas, Webb became fascinated by the news reports from the Mexican Revolution. The Texas Rangers played a major role in protecting the border from the insurrection, and their exploits had gained nationwide attention.

The approaching Texas Ranger centennial anniversary in 1935 gave Webb renewed vision for his idea to write the history of the Rangers. The men who fought the Indians, captured deadly outlaws, and protected the frontier told the best stories, so he conducted interviews. He also participated directly by going out on raids with the Rangers. Adjutant General Thomas F. Barton commissioned Webb an official Ranger.

Webb also made many friends among the Rangers, some of whom relished playing practical jokes on the balding professor. After a meal at a restaurant in West Texas, Webb's Ranger companions instructed the waitress to give the bill to the "professor," who had two dollars in his pocket. The waitress did as instructed. Webb decided to negotiate, asking the waitress, "How much will you take off for cash?" Her reply—"Everything but my shoes, Baldy"—earned the waitress a place in the history books and ensured Webb's status as somebody who could take a good joke. For his part, Webb gained an appreciation for the Rangers. He wrote: "Instead of having something—in this case courage—that most lack, they lack something that nearly everybody has. They lack fear."[5]

Webb went on to publish other books. His next,

The Great Plains, was hailed as a new interpretation of the American West, and Webb was awarded a PhD on the basis of the book's scholarship. Webb followed that book with another groundbreaking work, *The Great Frontier*. He wrote and edited more than twenty books.

Webb was married twice, first to Jane Oliphant, who died in 1960. The next year, he married Terrell Maverick, the widow of Maury Maverick, the former mayor of San Antonio and US congressman. Webb died March 8, 1963, in an automobile crash near Austin. His contributions to historical schools of thought are still debated in classrooms today, and his contribution to the legend of the Texas Rangers continues to be valuable.

Governor John B. Connally proclaimed Walter Prescott Webb eligible for interment in the Texas State Cemetery: "He embodied the best characteristics of a Texan in his personal qualities, and he devoted a lifetime to helping the remainder of the world understand the uniqueness of Texas."

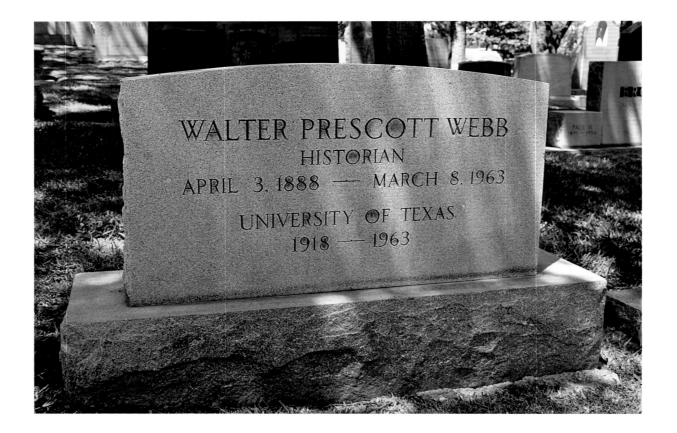

CHAPTER SEVEN

TEXAS
★
RANGERS

INTRODUCTION BY CAPTAIN JACK O'DAY DEAN

INTRODUCTION

BY CAPTAIN JACK O'DAY DEAN

Captain Jack O'Day Dean was a Texas Ranger for more than twenty years. Upon his retirement, he was appointed the United States Marshal, Western District of Texas, and he retired from this position in 2004. Captain Dean grew up north of Denton and went to Texas Christian University and Pan American University.

In the minds of Texans and non-Texans alike, the Texas Ranger remains the symbol of the Old West and of the state itself. The Ranger stands in the imagination as a solitary lawman bringing order to chaos with a quick wit and a revolver. His efficiency is defined in the old saying "One Ranger, one riot." Although not a factual representation of the Rangers, the image of the lone lawman is the common perception. Rangers can and have worked alone, but a majority of the time they worked with other Rangers, lawmen, soldiers, and settlers to help keep the peace in Texas.

The first Texas Rangers were little more than experienced frontiersmen hired by Stephen F. Austin as Indian fighters. Frontier defense and Indian fighting were to become a large part of the Texas Rangers' role in service to the state. Their job, however, was always more complex, always more nuanced than that of a soldier. General Zachary Taylor referred to the Rangers as his "eyes and ears" during the Mexican War.

Though a thoroughly modern law enforcement organization today, the Rangers' rich history and pedigree is perhaps unique in the world. The Rangers evolved with the state they served. Beginning as scouts and Indian fighters for the fledgling colonies, they served as soldiers during the Revolution,

A look down State Highway 165 to the Rose Gate entrance from 11th Street. Superintendent Harry Bradley had the flags placed along the highway in 1998. Photograph by Laurence Parent.

A view of the monument section of the Cemetery, the pond, and the footbridge that spans it. A monument to Gold Star Mothers, who have lost a child in war, and a monument honoring Congressional Medal of Honor recipients were erected in the area along with several military-themed monuments. Photograph by Laurence Parent.

protected the new Republic after San Jacinto, and fought alongside the United States Army in the Mexican War. Disbanded after the Civil War, they were reinstituted in the 1870s during some of Texas's darkest days to bring law and order to a mostly lawless frontier. Partly because of their own efficiency, they were made obsolete after the turn of the nineteenth century, when gunfighters were no longer needed to quell the Wild West. The Rangers changed with the times, implementing modern policing ideas.

The Rangers have been soldiers, policemen, Indian fighters, judges, ranchers, outlaws, politicians, and detectives, sometimes all at the same time throughout their more than one hundred and fifty years of existence. Falling in and out of favor in the Capitol, they came close to being disbanded in the 1930s until, in a reversal of fortune under Colonel Homer Garrison Jr., the Rangers were named a major division of the state police force.

Many of the most notable Texas Rangers from the past are interred at the Texas State Cemetery. In all, more than forty Rangers are buried at the Cemetery, from Stephen F. Austin, who founded the first Ranger corps, to Homer Garrison Jr., who revived the organization after a decade of decline. In between are some of the giant names of Texas history: Robert McAlpin "Three-Legged Willie" Williamson, Edward Burleson, William "Bigfoot" Wallace, and John Hughes. Modern Rangers and Ranger captains are buried right alongside their legendary brethren.

If you walk among the headstones on Republic Hill, you will find groups of Rangers buried next to each other in small clusters, but you will also find them next to lawmakers, authors, soldiers, governors, and others who made Texas what it is today. Even in the State Cemetery, the Rangers do not stand alone.

★

The Texas State Cemetery has several Texas Rangers buried on its grounds. Since their beginnings, they have set the standard for law enforcement in the state. Those buried at the Cemetery reflect the legend and mystique of the Rangers.

★

WILLIAM ALEXANDER ANDERSON "BIGFOOT" WALLACE

1817–1899

REPUBLIC HILL, SECTION 2 (C2), ROW K, PLOT 1

William Alexander Anderson Wallace, perhaps better known as "Bigfoot" Wallace, was one of the first Texas Rangers. Wallace spent his life on the frontiers of Texas. A survivor of the ill-fated Mier Expedition, the most disastrous of the raiding expeditions into Mexico in the early 1840s, he served as a captain in the Mexican War and drove a stagecoach from Austin to El Paso. Wallace, like Daniel Boone and Jim Bowie before him, occupies an exalted position on the roll of American heroes. Fanciful biographies written about Wallace throughout the twentieth century push the simple facts of his life into the arena of folklore—and the tales grew into legend perhaps with the assistance of Wallace himself.

Walter Prescott Webb, in his book *The Texas Rangers: A Century of Frontier Defense*, writes about Wallace, "His giant stature and childlike heart, his drollery and whimsicalness endeared him to the frontier people. His inexhaustible fund of anecdotes and a quaint style of narrative, unspoiled by courses of English composition, made him welcome by every fireside."[1]

What is known indisputably about Wallace's early years is that he was born in Lexington, Virginia, in 1817, to Andrew and Jane Anne Wallace. The Virginian Wallaces were said to be descendants of the Wallace Clan of Scotland, which claims Sir William Wallace, one of Scotland's greatest national heroes, as an ancestor.

Wallace was a large man for his time. An account of his life, published just before his death, said that he "in his prime was six feet two inches in his moccasins and weighed 240 pounds."[2] However, it was not his larger-than-life stature that earned Wallace his nickname.

A. J. Sowell, a contemporary, actually interviewed Wallace for "The Life of Bigfoot Wallace," published in 1899. Sowell records several variations on the story of the nickname's origin. One account held that Wallace received the name when he was imprisoned in Mexico during the Mier Expedition and his captors couldn't find shoes big enough to fit him. Another account was that he had killed a Comanche called "Big Foot" and had inherited the name from him.

Texas lore has it that Wallace moved to Texas in 1837 to join the fight against Mexico after his older brother and a cousin died at Goliad. He arrived too late but stayed in the area and was living near Austin in 1839, when it became the capital of the Republic. At the time, a Comanche with large feet was stealing horses and other property in the area. The Comanche left tracks

William Alexander Anderson
"Bigfoot" Wallace, Texas Ranger
and frontiersman, died in 1899
and was buried at the Texas State
Cemetery. Photograph used with
the permission of Texas State
Library and Archives Commission,
Archives and Information Services
Division, 1975/70-3683.

in the sand and Wallace tracked him several times, but was never able to apprehend him. In Sowell's account, Wallace said a man named Westfall killed the Comanche "on the Llano. I trailed him many times, and saw him three times at a distance, but never got a shot at him."[3] In a case of mistaken identity, Wallace was accused of the thefts by a settler named Gravis. Gravis followed the Comanche's big tracks to Wallace's house, but Wallace proved he was being wrongly accused when he compared his feet to the Comanche's tracks. But the story stuck, and so did the nickname.

Wallace joined Captain Jack Hays's Texas Rangers in 1840 and participated in various skirmishes with

Indians and Mexicans. In 1842, he was one of the many Texans who fought against Mexican General Adrián Woll and was a volunteer during the Somervell Expedition, a retaliatory mission against Mexican incursions into Texas. Alexander Somervell, under orders from President Sam Houston, attempted to invade Mexico, but he abandoned the plan and returned to Texas; many of his men, however, stayed behind with the intent to capture the Mexican town of Mier. Instead, Mexican forces captured them there. On the march to Mexico City, 176 men escaped, but they were recaptured within the week. Their Mexican captors decided to execute some of the escapees.

To determine who would die, the Mexicans devised a drawing, which came to be known as the "Black Bean Episode." An earthen pot containing 176 beans—all white except for 17 black ones—was passed among the captives. Wallace was one of the lucky ones: he picked a white bean and his life was spared. He was incarcerated in Mexico City until pleas from the governor of Virginia and from his father finally resulted in his release.

By 1845, Wallace had settled on the Medina River. He served again with the Texas Rangers under Jack Hays during the Mexican War. During the 1850s, Wallace and the Rangers fought border bandits as well as Indians on the Texas frontier. He served the same function during the Civil War.

J. Frank Dobie, a legendary chronicler of Texas folklore, wrote about Wallace:

His picturesqueness, humor, vitality, and representativeness of old-timy [*sic*] free days, free ways, and free land have broken down the literalness of every writer who has treated of him. Without directing events, he was there when they happened—and he was a tale-teller. As a folk hero he belongs more to social than to military history.[4]

Wallace died of pneumonia in 1899 and was buried in Devine, Texas, in Medina County. A month after his death, Wallace was moved to the Texas State Cemetery by an act of the Texas Legislature and buried at the feet of Stephen F. Austin.

ROBERT McALPIN "THREE-LEGGED WILLIE" WILLIAMSON

1804?–1859

REPUBLIC HILL, SECTION 2 (C2), ROW P, PLOT 6

Robert McAlpin "Three-Legged Willie" Williamson was a judge, Texas Ranger, and advocate for Texas independence. Williamson's story, like that of many early Texas settlers, has faded from fact and morphed into legend. Biographer Duncan W. Robinson wrote in his *Judge Robert McAlpin Williamson, Texas' Three-Legged Willie*, "Perhaps, too, the sober historian has been dismayed at the number of legends that cling to the man at every turn of his career, so that at times, it seems impossible to distinguish myth from fact."[5]

One thing about Williamson is sure and that is his nickname, "Three-Legged Willie." When Williamson was fifteen years old, he contracted what was then referred to as "white swelling," which may have been tuberculosis of the joints, and he was confined to his bed for several months. The lower half of his right leg drew up at the knee and was useless for the rest of his life. He later attached a wooden stump to his knee so that he could walk, giving him three "legs."

One of the more colorful legends clinging to Williamson establishes him as a master of the rebuttal. In 1837, Republic of Texas district judges were assigned places of jurisdiction and traveled there to administer the law. Williamson's assignment was Shelby County, a notorious haven for outlaws from all over the United States and beyond. When it was made known that Williamson was going to hold court, a group of Shelby County citizens met and decided they would not submit to the new Republic's court.

There are several variants of the story, but Robinson delivers an account of the tale he deems most probable. Williamson sat behind a dry-goods box while the sheriff of the county announced that court was in session. Soon after, a "tall, unkempt ruffian" informed Williamson of the citizens' decision. A confrontation ensued, and as Robinson describes it:

> Looking mildly at the man, Williamson asked: "What legal authority can you give for such a procedure?" Quickly drawing a Bowie knife from his belt and slamming it on the box before Williamson, the spokesman for the frontier snarled, "This, sir, is the law in Shelby County!" In a flash Williamson whipped out a long-barreled pistol. "If that is the law of Shelby County," he thundered, "this is the constitution that overrides all law!" Placing the pistol beside the dagger, he turned to the sheriff. "Mr. Sheriff," he ordered, "you will please call the grand jury." The representative of "the people" slunk out of the courtroom, and the session proceeded.[6]

Legends aside, Williamson contributed much to the establishment of Texas as a republic and was an ardent advocate of its annexation to the United States. Some historians might go so far as to say Williamson was the loudest voice in the argument for a revolution in Texas.

In fact, Williamson was arrested for expressing his opinions after delivering an incendiary speech in San

Robert McAlpin "Three-Legged Willie" Williamson, Texas Republic–era judge and Texas Ranger, died in 1859 and was buried in Wharton, Texas, but was interred at the Texas State Cemetery through the efforts of Louis W. Kemp in 1930. Used with the permission of Texas State Library and Archives Commission, Archives and Information Services Division, 1992/8-1.

Felipe on July 4, 1835. He was one of the heads of the war party—along with William Barrett Travis and Samuel May Williams—who called for armed rebellion against Mexico. In his speech, he said the colonists had no choice but to pursue the "taking of San Antonio." His closing battle cry—"Liberty or Death should be our determination, and let us one and all unite to protect our country from all invasion"—earned Williamson another nickname: the Patrick Henry of Texas. The speech was published in Brazoria and distributed throughout the colonies. When Mexican officials read it, they ordered Williamson arrested. The speech ensured the abandonment of virtually all hope of a peaceful resolution of problems with Mexico. A wanted man, Williamson fled to the town of Mina to avoid capture.

While there, he was commissioned to lead a corps of Rangers, which he commanded, to guard the Texas frontier during the war. This corps was the precursor of the present-day Texas Rangers. Williamson's Rangers protected the frontier from invasion throughout the war for independence, despite the fact that their leader had been summoned to serve in a cavalry unit at the Battle of San Jacinto.

After the war, Williamson served in the Republic of Texas House of Representatives in the Fifth, Sixth, and Seventh Congress, in the Republic of Texas Senate in the Eighth Congress, and in the House again in the Ninth Congress. Following Texas's annexation to the United States, Williamson continued his career in public service as a senator in the first two state legislatures. He retired to private life in March 1850 and died in Wharton in 1859 after a long illness. He was reinterred in the State Cemetery through the efforts of historian Louis W. Kemp. When Williamson's remains were brought to the Cemetery in 1930, a special joint session of the legislature was convened in his honor.

JOHN REYNOLDS HUGHES

1855–1947

REPUBLIC HILL, SECTION 2 (C2), ROW S, PLOT 15

John Reynolds Hughes served as a Texas Ranger from 1887 to 1915, the longest-serving Ranger captain in the history of the agency. Known as the "Border Boss," Hughes had a legendary reputation for his work along the Mexican border and was immortalized by author Zane Grey in his novel *The Lone Star Ranger*. Gray modeled the hero of his book after Hughes and dedicated it to Hughes and the Texas Rangers.

Legendary outlaws and gunslingers, such as John Wesley Hardin, roamed West Texas during Hughes's time as a Ranger. But also during his long tenure with the organization, Hughes saw the Texas frontier change from a haven for bandits to a stable place with thriving urban areas and prosperous rural regions. The Rangers transformed, too, from a quasi-military unit to a modern law enforcement agency.

Hughes was born in Henry County, Illinois, in 1855. Although his education was informal, Hughes possessed what we would call today "street smarts." By age fourteen, he was working on a cattle ranch, but he soon moved to the Indian Territory, where he lived among the Choctaw and the Osage tribes. By 1874, Hughes was living among the Comanche Indian tribe in the Southwest. It is said he traded in the Fort Sill area and became friends with the Comanche chief Quanah Parker. Hughes also worked as a cowboy on the Chisholm Trail.

Hughes bought a farm near Liberty Hill, Texas. In 1886, he tracked a group of horse thieves to New Mexico, reportedly killing a few along the way. He captured the rest and brought the horses back to their rightful owners. The dramatic pursuit brought Hughes to the

attention of the Texas Rangers, and he was invited to join the organization in August 1887. He was assigned to Company D, Frontier Battalion, at Camp Wood on the Nueces River.

Hughes demonstrated his superior skill as a tracker and scout throughout his early career and was often assigned to long solo expeditions or to expeditions accompanied by only one or two other Rangers. He served with the notorious Bass Outlaw before Outlaw was expelled from the Rangers for threatening a sheriff in Alpine. After Outlaw's departure, Hughes was promoted to sergeant.

He continued to rise in the organization, earning his promotion to the coveted position of captain in June 1893. He replaced Ranger Captain Frank Jones, who had been killed in a shoot-out with Mexican bandits at Pirate Island on the Rio Grande.

In 1900, the state legislature abolished the Rangers as a frontier battalion and reorganized the group as a state agency. The new Rangers were divided into four battalions, with Hughes appointed the captain of Company D. He retired from the Texas Rangers in 1915, but not before being promoted to senior captain. He continued to be active after retirement and enjoyed a career in the banking industry and as chairman of the board of directors for the Citizens Industrial Bank of Austin.

Hughes was the first recipient of the Certificate of Valor, an award given to law enforcement officers in recognition of bravery. He had his own definition of bravery, believing it to be a trait that should

be tempered with caution. He always instructed new recruits in his philosophy: "Nerve without judgment is dangerous," he would say, "and has no place in the Ranger Service."[7]

He gained more publicity late in life in a now-famous photograph that epitomized the old and the new in law enforcement: Hughes, by this time an elderly man, sits astride a horse and is in conversation with a younger policeman on a motorcycle.

John Reynolds Hughes remained a man of determination until the very end. He died at the age of ninety-three on June 3, 1947, from a self-inflicted gunshot wound. It was speculated that he was in poor health and did not want to be a burden on his family. He was interred at the Texas State Cemetery for his lifetime of service to Texas law enforcement. A gray granite headstone was erected on Hughes's grave in 1970 bearing the inscription: "Noted for ability, courage, firmness."

Texas Ranger John Hughes, later in life, on a visit to the Texas Department of Public Safety barracks. Courtesy of the Texas Ranger Hall of Fame, Waco.

Photograph by Will Erwin

THE TEXAS RANGER'S PRAYER

O GOD, WHOSE END IS JUSTICE,
WHOSE STRENGTH IS ALL OUR STAY,
BE NEAR AND BLESS MY MISSION
AS I GO FORTH TODAY.
LET WISDOM GUIDE MY ACTIONS,
LET COURAGE FILL MY HEART
AND HELP ME LORD, IN EVERY HOUR
TO DO A RANGER'S PART.
PROTECT WHEN DANGER THREATENS,
SUSTAIN WHEN TRAILS ARE ROUGH;
HELP ME TO KEEP MY STANDARD HIGH
AND SMILE AT EACH REBUFF.

WHEN NIGHT COMES DOWN UPON ME,
I PRAY THEE LORD BE NIGH.
WHETHER ON LONELY SCOUT, OR CAMPED,
UNDER THE TEXAS SKY.
KEEP ME, O GOD, IN LIFE
AND WHEN MY DAYS SHALL END,
FORGIVE MY SINS AND TAKE ME IN,
FOR JESUS SAKE, AMEN.

COLLIER READ GRANBERRY
JUNE 29, 1899 — AUGUST 23, 1962
EXECUTIVE DIRECTOR, TEXAS LEGISLATIVE COUNCIL 1950-1962
PARLIAMENTARIAN TEXAS HOUSE OF REPRESENTATIVES 19 SESSIONS
PROFESSOR OF ELECTRICAL ENGINEERING
THE UNIVERSITY OF TEXAS 1930-1954
MEMBER OF ELECTRICAL ENGINEERING STAFF 1921-1954
ASSISTANT TO THE PRESIDENT 1947-1950
ASSISTANT TO THE CHANCELLOR 1950-1955, THE UNIVERSITY OF TEXAS
HIS WIFE
RUTH McMILLAN GRANBERRY

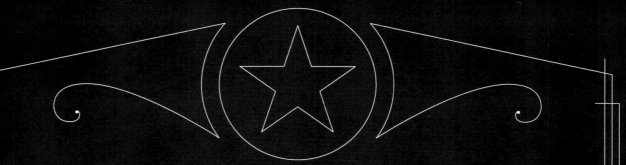

EPILOGUE

★

GOVERNOR RICK PERRY

EPILOGUE

BY GOVERNOR RICK PERRY

Governor Rick Perry began his political career in the Texas House of Representatives and later served as agriculture commissioner and lieutenant governor. The longest-serving governor in Texas history, he is the first Texas A&M graduate to serve in that office.

Texas is a land of legends, where notable men and women of the past always seem to loom larger than life. Search the history books of any other state in America and you will be hard-pressed to find a figure that matches the gravitas of Houston, the courage of Travis, the magnetism of Rayburn, or the colorful personas of Ma and Pa Ferguson.

Our history is a tremendous source of pride for all who call Texas home, and something that sets Texas apart from, and above, every other state.

But keeping our history alive for future Texans is important for reasons that go far beyond state pride. It is from the pages of Texas history, filled with the extraordinary deeds of ordinary men and women, that a new generation glimpses the power of the Texas spirit—that indomitable sense of optimism that allows a young Texan of the most meager circumstances to dream the greatest of dreams. And in studying the lives and legacies of Texas's foremost leaders, the student learns the very essence of what it means to be a Texan: strong but gentle, compassionate to those in need, and unafraid to stand for what you believe in.

That is why preserving, remembering, and honoring our history is essential for the future of our state. The Texas State Cemetery, as the only state-funded cemetery in America dedicated to honoring those who have made significant contributions to society, is an integral part of Texas's historical preservation efforts and is bringing history to life for future generations.

The previous pages capture a few notable moments in Texas history and bring them to life through the words and memories of history's authors. My hope is that these stories will give every reader a deeper affection for the state we love.

NOTES

1. HISTORY OF THE CEMETERY

1. "Proceedings of the Senate and House of Representatives Of the Legislature of Texas, On the Occasion of the Death of General Edward Burleson, which Occurred December 26, 1851" (Austin: State Gazette Office, Cushey and Hampton, 1851), 4–5.

2. Douglas K. Boyd, *Confederate Veterans at Rest: Archeological and Bioarcheological Investigations at the Texas State Cemetery, Travis County, Texas, Reports of Investigations*, No. 107 (Austin: Prewitt and Associates, Inc., 1996), 29.

2. REPUBLIC OF TEXAS

1. *Moses and Stephen F. Austin Papers*, 1676, 1765–1889 (Briscoe Center for American History, University of Texas at Austin).

2. Ron Tyler, ed., *The Handbook of Texas* (Austin: Texas State Historical Association, 1996), 297.

3. J. Frank Dobie, *Tales of Old-Time Texas* (Austin: University of Texas Press, 1984), 38.

4. Ibid., 41.

5. Ibid.

3. CIVIL WAR AND RECONSTRUCTION

1. Charles P. Roland, *Albert Sidney Johnston: Soldier of Three Republics* (Austin: University of Texas Press, 1964), 353.

2. Ibid., 5.

3. Ibid., 46.

4. Stanley S. McGowen, "Augustus Buchel: A Forgotten Texas Patriot," *Military History of the West*, vol. 25, no. 1 (Spring 1995), 1.

5. Tyler, *The Handbook of Texas*, 75.

4. PUBLIC OFFICIALS

1. "Proceedings of the Senate and House of Representatives Of the Legislature of Texas, On the Occasion of the Death of General Edward Burleson, which Occurred December 26, 1851" (Austin: State Gazette Office, Cushey and Hampton, 1851), 29.

2. May Nelson Paulissen and Carl McQueary, *Miriam: The Southern Belle Who Became the First Woman Governor of Texas* (Austin: Eakin Press, 1995), 114.

3. Robert G. Winchester, *James Pinckney Henderson: Texas' First Governor* (San Antonio: Naylor Publishing, 1971), 17.

4. Max Sherman, ed., *Barbara Jordan: Speaking the Truth with Eloquent Thunder* (Austin: University of Texas Press, 2007), 27.

5. Ibid., 39.

6. Ibid.

7. Ibid., 41.

8. Barbara Boxer, "Life of Barbara Jordan," *Congressional Record*, January 22, 1996.

9. Sheila Jackson-Lee, "Tribute to the Late Hon. Barbara Jordan," *Congressional Record*, January 24, 1996.

10. Kent Biffle, "Ex-Gov. John Connally Dies at 76," *Dallas Morning News*, June 16, 1993.

11. Paul Burka, "Remembering Jim Mattox," *Texas Monthly*, December 2008.

12. Molly Ivins, "Remembering Ann Richards," www.creators.com/opinion/molly-ivins/remembering-ann-richards.html, 2006.

13. Kelly Shannon, "Ann Richards Dies of Cancer at 73," Associated Press, September 14, 2006.

5. CULTURAL FIGURES

1. Tyler, *The Handbook of Texas*, 662–663.

2. Mike Cox, *Fred Gipson: Texas Storyteller* (Austin: Shoal Creek Publishing, 1980), ix.

3. Ibid., 46.

4. Ibid., 139.

5. Buck O'Neil, with Steve Wulf and David Conrads, *I Was Right on Time* (New York: Simon & Schuster, 1996), 144.

6. James A. Riley, *Dandy, Day, and the Devil* (Cocoa, FL: TK Publishers, 1987), 108–109.

7. J. Frank Dobie, *Guide to Life and Literature of the Southwest* (Charleston, SC: BiblioBazaar, 2006), 160.

6. EDUCATORS AND ACADEMICS

1. Ken Herman and Mary Ann Rosner, "Keeton, Long-time UT Law Dean, Dies," *Austin American-Statesman*, January 11, 1999.

2. Governor's Proclamation, signed by Dolph Briscoe, December 20, 1974 (Texas State Cemetery vertical files, Keeton).

3. Ibid.

4. Ibid.

5. Necah S. Furman, *Walter Prescott Webb: His Life and Impact* (Albuquerque: University of New Mexico Press, 1976), 115.

7. TEXAS RANGERS

1. Walter Prescott Webb, *The Texas Rangers: A Century of Frontier Defense*, 2nd ed. (Austin: University of Texas Press, 1965), 87.

2. Tyler, *The Handbook of Texas*, 808.

3. A. J. Sowell, "The Life of Bigfoot Wallace," *Frontier Times* (1927), 55.

4. Webb, *The Texas Rangers*, 856.

5. Duncan W. Robinson, *Judge Robert McAlpin Williamson, Texas' Three-Legged Willie* (Austin: Texas State Historical Association, 1948), 230.

6. Ibid., 155.

7. William Warren Sterling, *Trails and Trials of a Texas Ranger* (Norman: University of Oklahoma Press, 1959), 386.

BIBLIOGRAPHY

Arthur, Dora Fowler. "General J. Pinckney Henderson." *Texas Magazine*, vol. 1, no. 12 (April 1897): 387–395.

Ashman, Charles R. *Connally: The Adventures of Big Bad John.* New York: Morrow Publishing, 1974.

Barker, Eugene C. *The Life of Stephen F. Austin: Founder of Texas, 1793–1836.* Austin: Texas State Historical Association, 1949.

Beach, Patrick. "The King of Texas." *Austin American-Statesman*, December 6, 1998.

Beach, Patrick, and Ken Herman. "A Texas Giant Is Gone." *Austin American-Statesman*, June 19, 1999.

Biffle, Kent. "Ex-Gov. John Connally Dies at 76." *Dallas Morning News*, June 16, 1993.

Blackburn, J. K. P., L. B. Giles, and E. S. Dodd. *Terry Texas Ranger Trilogy.* Austin: State House Press, 1996.

Boxer, Barbara. "Life of Barbara Jordan." *Congressional Record*, January 22, 1996.

Boyd, Douglas K. *Confederate Veterans at Rest: Archeological and Bioarcheological Investigations at the Texas State Cemetery, Travis County, Texas, Reports of Investigations*, No. 107. Austin: Prewitt and Associates, Inc., 1996.

Bradford, Brownie. "Waller Had Colorful Career." *American Statesman-Sunday Magazine*, June 10, 1928.

Burka, Paul. "The Dominator." *Texas Monthly* (August 1999): 9–14.

———. "Remembering Jim Mattox." *Texas Monthly* (December 2008).

Cantrell, Gregg. *Stephen F. Austin: Empresario of Texas.* New Haven and London: Yale University Press, 1999.

Clark, James A. *Three Stars for the Colonel: The Biography of Ernest O. Thompson.* New York: Random House, 1954.

Clopton, Mildred. "Capital City's 1st Mayor Lies in State Cemetery." *Austin American-Statesman*, December 12, 1954.

Connally, John B. *In History's Shadow: An American Odyssey.* New York: Hyperion Publishing, 1993.

Cox, Mike. *Fred Gipson: Texas Storyteller.* Austin: Shoal Creek Publishing, 1980.

Crawford, Ann Fears, and Crystal Sasse Ragsdale. *Women in Texas.* Austin: State House Press, 1992.

Dobie, J. Frank. *Guide to Life and Literature of the Southwest.* Charleston, SC: BiblioBazaar, 2006.

———. *Tales of Old-Time Texas.* Austin: University of Texas Press, 1984.

Estes, Adella Lamartine. *Lamar Letters.* http://txgenelady.com/LamarFamily/LamarLetters.html.

"Final Curtain Drops for Golden Girl." *Amarillo Daily News*, October 9, 1952.

Fischer, Ernest G. *Robert Potter: Founder of the Texas Navy.* Gretna, LA: Pelican Publishing, 1976.

Friend, Llerena B. *Sam Houston: The Great Designer.* Austin: University of Texas Press, 1989.

Furman, Necah S. *Walter Prescott Webb: His Life and Impact.* Albuquerque: University of New Mexico Press, 1976.

Gallaway, B. P., ed. *Texas, the Dark Corner of the Confederacy: Contemporary Accounts of the Lone Star State in the Civil War.* Lincoln: University of Nebraska, 1994.

Gardner, William H. "Texas Governors: Francis R. Lubbock." *Houston Post*, October 1, 1958.

Governor's Proclamation, signed by Dolph Briscoe, December 20, 1974. Texas State Cemetery vertical files, Keeton.

Governor's Proclamation, signed by John Connally, March 11, 1963. Texas State Cemetery vertical files, Webb.

Gray, Ronald N. "Edmund J. Davis: Radical Republican and Reconstruction Governor of Texas." PhD diss., Texas Tech University, 1976.

Harmon, Dave, and Dave McNeely. "Former Texas House Speaker Recalled as Eloquent Orator." *Austin American-Statesman*, March 8, 2000.

Hart, Katherine. "Austin's Growth Began With Waller." *Austin American-Statesman*, August 2, 1969.

Heinsohn, Edmund. "Funeral Oration at the Services for May Peterson Thompson." Texas State Cemetery vertical files.

Herman, Ken, and Mary Ann Rosner. "Keeton, Longtime UT Law Dean, Dies." *Austin American-Statesman*, January 11, 1999.

Ivins, Molly. "Remembering Ann Richards." www.creators .com/opinion/molly-ivins/remembering-ann-richards .html, 2006.

Jackson-Lee, Sheila. "Tribute to the Late Hon. Barbara Jordan." *Congressional Record*, January 24, 1996.

Jenkins, John H., and Kenneth Kesselus. *Edward Burleson: Texas Frontier Leader*. Austin: Jenkins Publishing, 1990.

Kinch, Sam, and Stuart Long. *Allan Shivers: The Pied Piper of Texas Politics*. Austin: Shoal Creek Publishing, 1973.

Lich, Glen E. *Fred Gipson at Work*. College Station: Texas A&M University Press, 1990.

Lincecum, Jerry B., and Edward H. Phillips, eds. *Adventures of a Frontier Naturalist: The Life and Times of Dr. Gideon Lincecum*. College Station: Texas A&M University Press, 1994.

Lone Star Junction, *Archives War*. www.lsjunction.com/events/ archives.htm.

————. *Francis R. Lubbock, 1815–1905*. www.lsjunction.com/ people/lubbock.htm.

————. *Runaway Scrape*. www.lsjunction.com/events/runaway .htm.

Lubbock, Francis Richard. *Six Decades in Texas*. Ed. C. W. Raines. Austin: Ben Jones and Co. Printers, 1900.

McCampbell, Ward. "Biographical Essay, Thomas William Ward." Austin History Center, Biographical File, March 1964.

McGowen, Stanley S. "Augustus Buchel: A Forgotten Texas Patriot." *Military History of the West*, vol. 25, no. 1 (Spring 1995): 1–21.

Mathis, Nancy. "She Trotted her Horse, Made a Path Wide, Deep." *Houston Chronicle*, January 20, 1996.

Moses and Stephen F. Austin Papers, 1676, 1765–1889. Briscoe Center for American History, University of Texas at Austin.

Nunn, Annie Dyer. "May Peterson." *Amarillo Sunday News and Globe*, July 24, 1927.

O'Neil, Buck, with Steve Wulf and David Conrads. *I Was Right on Time*. New York: Simon & Schuster, 1996.

Paulissen, May Nelson, and Carl McQueary. *Miriam: The Southern Belle Who Became the First Woman Governor of Texas*. Austin: Eakin Press, 1995.

Pope, Henry David. *A Lady and a Lone Star Flag*, 2nd ed. Bryan, Texas: Brazos Valley Printing, 1986.

Prindle, David F. *Petroleum Politics and the Texas Railroad Commission*. Austin: University of Texas Press, 1981.

"Proceedings of the Senate and House of Representatives Of the Legislature of Texas, On the Occasion of the Death of General Edward Burleson, which Occurred December 26, 1851." Austin: State Gazette Office, Cushey and Hampton, 1851.

Ratcliffe, R. G., and Ann Marie Killday. "Ann Richards." *Houston Chronicle*, September 14, 2006.

"Reminiscences of Judge Edwin Waller." *Quarterly of the Texas State Historical Association*, vol. IV (July 1900–April 1901): 33–36.

Riley, James A. *Dandy, Day, and the Devil*. Cocoa, FL: TK Publishers, 1987.

Robertson, David W., David A. Anderson, and Charles Alan Wright. *In Memoriam, W. Page Keeton*. www.utexas.edu/faculty/ council/1999-2000/memorials/Keeton/keeton.html.

Robinson, Charles M. *The Men Who Wear the Star: The Story of the Texas Rangers*. New York: Random House, 2000.

Robinson, Duncan W. *Judge Robert McAlpin Williamson, Texas' Three-Legged Willie*. Austin: Texas State Historical Association, 1948.

Rogers, Mary Beth. *Barbara Jordan: American Hero*. New York: Bantam, 2000.

Roland, Charles P. *Albert Sidney Johnston: Soldier of Three Republics*. Austin: University of Texas Press, 1964.

Rutherford, Bruce, *Ferguson: The Impeachment of Jim Ferguson*. Austin: Eakin Press, 1983.

Sam Houston Memorial Museum. *Flags of the Republic*. www .shsu.edu/~smm_www/FunStuff/RepublicFlags/Dodson .shtml.

Scarborough, Megan. *A Voice That Could Not Be Stilled: Barbara Jordan's Legacy of Equality and Justice*. www.utexas.edu/features/ archive/2003/jordan.html.

Scott, Paul R. *John A. Wharton: The Forgotten General*. Terry's Texas Rangers Online Archive. www.terrystexasrangers .org/biography/submitted/wharton.html.

Sexton, F. B. "J. Pinckney Henderson. An Address Delivered on the Occasion of the Obsequies in Memory of General Henderson, August 21st, 1858." *Southwestern Historical Quarterly* Online, vol. 001, no. 3: 187–203. *www.tshaonline.org/ publications/journals/shq/online/v001/n3/article_6.html*.

Shannon, Kelly. "Ann Richards Dies of Cancer at 73." Associated Press, September 14, 2006.

Sherman, Max, ed. *Barbara Jordan: Speaking the Truth with Eloquent Thunder*. Austin: University of Texas Press, 2007.

Silverthorne, Elizabeth. *Ashbel Smith of Texas: Pioneer, Patriot, Statesman, 1805–1886*. College Station: Texas A&M University Press, 1982.

Smithwick, Noah. *The Evolution of a State, or, Recollections of Old Texas Days*. Austin: Gammel Book Company, 1900.

Sowell, A. J. "The Life of Bigfoot Wallace." *Frontier Times*, 1927.

Sterling, William Warren. *Trails and Trials of a Texas Ranger*. Norman: University of Oklahoma Press, 1959.

Stockdale, Fletcher S. "Eulogy of Augustus Buchel by Lieutenant Governor Fletcher S. Stockdale, May 10, 1865." Fletcher Stockdale Collection, Texas State Library and Archives Commission.

Terrell, Charles Vernon. *The Terrells and 85 Years of Texas, from Indians to Atomic Bomb*. Austin, 1948.

Texas Railroad Commission. *The Railroad Commission of Texas: An Informal History Compiled for Its Centennial (April 1991)*. www.rrc.state.tx.us/about/history/centennial/centennialtoc.php.

Texas State Library & Archives Commission. *Anson Jones to J. Pinckney Henderson*, February 15, 1844. www.tsl.state.tx.us/treasures/giants/jones/jones-henderson-feb44-1.html.

———. *Forever Free*: Nineteenth-Century African-American Legislators and Constitutional Convention Delegates of Texas. www.tsl.state.tx.us/exhibits/forever.

———. *Hazardous Business: Industry, Regulation, and the Texas Railroad Commission*. www.tsl.state.tx.us/exhibits/railroad/intro.html.

Tinkle, Lon. *An American Original: The Life of J. Frank Dobie*. Austin: University of Texas Press, 1983.

Tyler, Ron, ed. *The Handbook of Texas*. Austin: Texas State Historical Association, 1996.

Vestal, Stanley. *Bigfoot Wallace: A Biography*. Boston: Houghton Mifflin, 1942.

Webb, Walter Prescott. *The Texas Rangers: A Century of Frontier Defense*, 2nd ed. Austin: University of Texas Press, 1965.

———, ed. *The Handbook of Texas in Two Volumes*. Austin: Texas State Historical Association, 1952.

Winchester, Robert G. *James Pinckney Henderson: Texas' First Governor*. San Antonio: Naylor Publishing, 1971.

Wooster, Ralph A. *Lone Star Generals in Gray*. Austin: Eakin Press, 2000.

———. *Lone Star Blue and Gray: Essays on Texas in the Civil War*. Austin: Texas State Historical Association, 1995.

GENERAL INFORMATION

The Texas State Cemetery is located at 909 Navasota Street in Austin. The Visitor Center is open from 8 a.m. to 5 p.m. Monday through Friday. The State Cemetery Grounds are open to the public 365 days a year, 8 a.m. to 5 p.m.

PHONE NUMBERS

Cemetery
(512) 463-0605

Tour Reservations
(512) 463-6600

Superintendent Harry Bradley
(512) 463-6023, (512) 415-4901

WEBSITE

www.cemetery.state.tx.us

E-MAIL

StateCemetery@tfc.state.tx.us

MAILING ADDRESS

Texas State Cemetery
909 Navasota Street
Austin, TX 78702

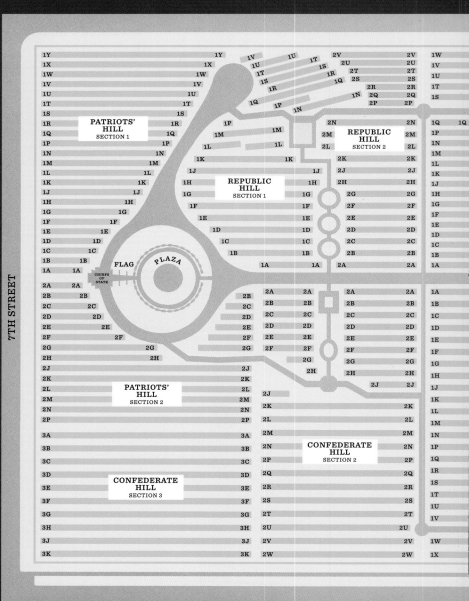

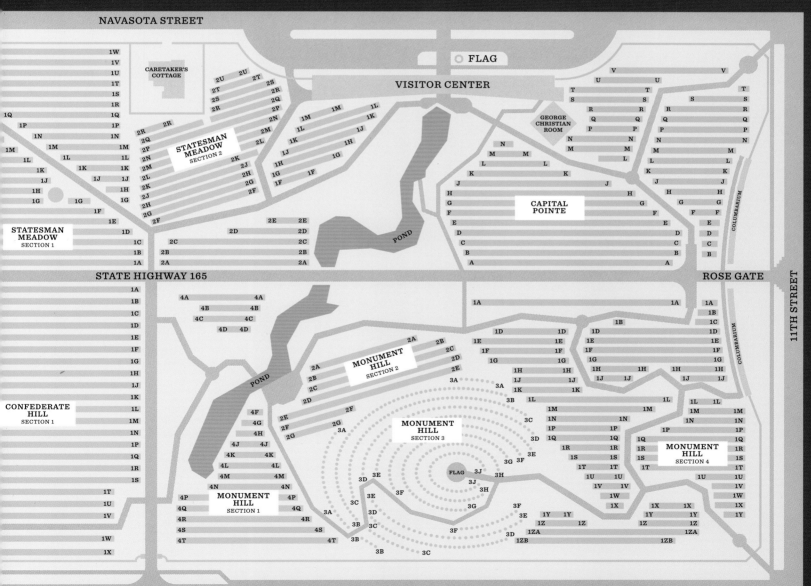

INDEX